Keep Talking

Keep Talking

A MOTHER-DAUGHTER GUIDE
TO THE PRETEEN YEARS

LYNDA MADISON, PH.D.

Andrews and McMeel
A Universal Press Syndicate Company
Kansas City

www.andrewsmcmeel.com

99 00 01 02 03 RDH 10 9 8 7 6 5 4 3 2

A hardcover edition of this book was published in 1997 by Andrews McMeel Publishing.

Library of Congress Cataloging-in-Publication Data
As Catalogued for the Hardcover Version
Madison, Lynda.
    Keep talking : a mother-daughter guide to the pre-teen years /
Lynda Madison.
      p.   cm.
    ISBN 0-8362-8736-3 (ppb)
    1. Teenage girls. 2. Mothers and daughters. 3. Communication in the
family. I. Title.
HQ798.M2944   1997
306.874'3—dc21   95-52078
                                                                        CIP

Book design and composition by Top Dog Design

Illustrations by Lynda Madison, Ph.D.

The views expressed herein are not necessarily those of the staff or management of Children's Hospital, Omaha.

The individuals depicted in this book are composite characters drawn from my life experiences and client contacts. Any resemblance to real individuals is purely coincidental. The circumstances presented are real, but names and other identifying information have been changed to conceal actual identities.

——————— ATTENTION: SCHOOLS AND BUSINESSES ———————
Andrews and McMeel books are available at quantity discounts with bulk purchase for educational, business, or sales promotional use. For information, please write to: Special Sales Department, Andrews and McMeel, 4520 Main Street, Kansas City, Missouri 64111-7701.

To my parents,

Max and Elvira Sallach,

for their many

contributions to my person

CONTENTS

PREFACE

Even though this book was designed with mothers and daughters in mind, I recognize that there are families with no mother present or in which the person who will take the time to read this book with the daughter is not her mother. In these special circumstances, some of the exercises will not apply; a few will need to be modified or left out. However, the purpose of the book is to help establish for any preteen girl a closer relationship with a significant adult who can help prepare her for growing up.

ACKNOWLEDGMENTS

If you find value in reading this book, it comes not just from me but from the many people who have touched my life. I am particularly grateful to my husband, Jim, and my daughters, Megan and Audrey, for their ongoing reading and encouragement of this book and for freeing me for countless hours of writing. I thank my mother and dear friend for bringing her special sensibilities to the reading of this manuscript. I give special appreciation to the following people for reading and/or making suggestions for this book: Ann Matzke; Mary Fran Flood; Natalie Gendler; Mary Legino and her daughters, Allison and Kristen; Margaret Krusen; Joanie Young and her daughter, Katy; Michele Marsh and her daughter, Margaret; and Megan Minturn. I also am grateful to all the mother-daughter pairs I met through my professional work who helped to educate me about this special relationship. And I offer thanks to my agent, Frank Weimann, and my editor, Jake Morrissey, for believing in this book and making it possible.

Keep Talking

INTRODUCTION

Notes to Mother and Daughter

Dear Mother:

YOUR DAUGHTER will learn many things from other people during her adolescent years. Her thinking will be influenced by teachers, peers, books, movies, television, and music. She will learn a lot about puberty from friends, but not all of their information will be accurate or complete. She will learn a lot about relationships from the media, but often not how you hope she will behave. From all these sources, she will have to sort out how to make decisions, value friendships, and respect herself. As a mother, you may wonder where you fit into your daughter's education about life. You won't want to simply hang on for the ride as she enters the teen years. You care about her and want to understand her experiences so she learns the right things at the right time. And you want to counter the negative influences you know she will face as she grows up.

As a psychologist, I have had many opportunities to see how important mothers are for their daughters, especially as those daughters begin the transition to becoming a woman. As a mother, I know the joy of feeling close to my own daughters as they learn about themselves and the world. But I also know how frightening it can be to think of all the challenges girls face today and how hard it can be to know the best way to help your daughter grow.

This book is designed to help you and your daughter feel comfortable talking together about growing up. It includes information and exercises that can help you develop a healthy relationship and build a foundation for future discussions. Discussing the facts of life is only one of the conversations you will want to have with your daughter, and this book does not include That Talk. It leaves some topics for you to discuss later. This book introduces the physical changes for which your daughter needs to be ready, and discusses these along with other important issues she will face as she grows up. To get the most benefit from this book, you should read it and do the exercises *together.*

The book starts out with less complex issues, then tackles more difficult ones in later chapters. It can be used in many different ways. Younger girls will be most interested in the earlier parts of the book and may want you to focus mainly on the exercises. When they get to a point in the book where the material is ahead of their experiences, you may want to set it aside for a while. Older girls will want to read the text all the way through with you. Even after you have finished the book, you may want to refer back to it at times to help you discuss important issues as they come up.

However you use this book, remember that the goal is to listen and talk to each other, so take your time. I suggest that you read one chapter or part of a chapter at a time to give you and your daughter the opportunity to discuss and practice the things you learn. Don't feel that you have to do absolutely every exercise, but also try not to hurry through the exercises. Be comfortable with periods of silence as you each think about your answers. And feel free to go off on tangents if your daughter wants to talk about other issues. Listening to each other is more important than finishing this book according to some arbitrary schedule. Remember that time is the best gift you can give your daughter and yourself—time in which you are available for information, support, and guidance.

Dear Daughter:

YOU ARE GOING to be a teenager—or an adolescent, as many grown-ups call it. Maybe not for a year or so, but it will happen sooner than you think. Do you ever wonder what growing up will be like, but not know how to find out more about it? Maybe you have noticed changes in your body or feelings that make you wonder if you are already on your way. You might have heard other girls talking or seen things in movies you have wondered about. Even if you don't have questions right now, you probably will pretty soon. And your mother will want to help answer them. Reading this book is a good way to start discussing a lot of things with your mother. I hope you will feel comfortable talking to her all the way through your teen years.

CHAPTER 1

Getting to Know You

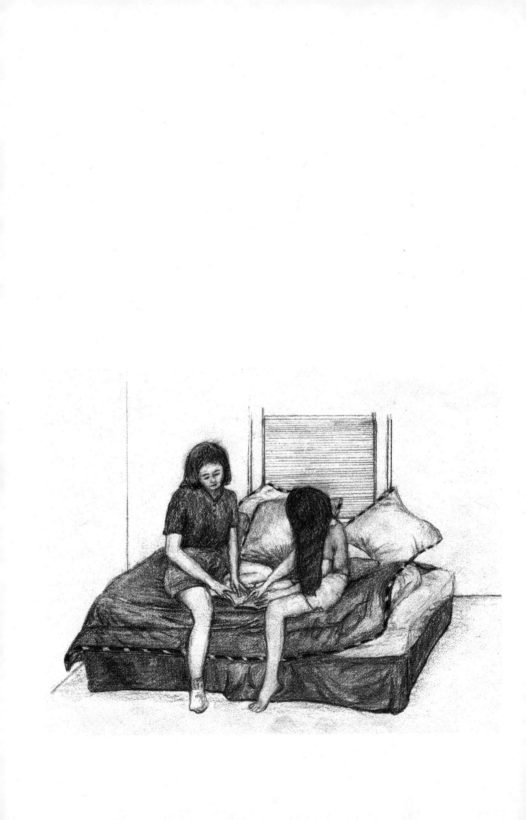

Mother and Daughter Together

ARE YOU SITTING next to each other? Are you comfortable? Great! When mothers and daughters sit down to read together, good things happen. They relax instead of rushing around. They talk to each other. And usually they get to know each other better. Getting to know each other may seem like a silly idea. After all, you've been together since you were a baby. But you will be surprised as you read this book how much you will learn about each other.

Why is this book for mothers and daughters instead of fathers and daughters? Not because it's a secret or because fathers shouldn't know the information in it. In fact, it might be a good idea if your father does read it. He is a great person to talk to about growing up and getting along with others—especially boys, since he was one. But this particular book is for mothers and daughters because nobody else shares exactly what you do.

You have a lot in common because you are female. You start out a girl, and you end up a woman. And a lot of changes happen in between—changes in your body, your feelings, your friends, and your plans for the future. Of course you don't need to think about all these changes at once. But eventually, just because you get older, they will happen, and you will become a grown woman.

As mother and daughter, you have already spent a lot of time together, and you will be together for many years to come. You are part of a family and you care a great deal about each other. When it comes to getting through the adolescent years, you both have the same goal in mind—for you eventually to become a grown-up. Not just any grown-up, either, but a grown-up woman who is comfortable with her body, able to make and keep friends, and able to make good decisions on the way to reaching her goals. What better person is there to learn from than your mother? She has been along that road herself. She cares about you and wants to help if you need her.

As a psychologist, I often talk to large groups of mothers and preteen daughters together. When I ask if they are excited about the coming teen years, about half of them raise their hands. When I ask who is a little nervous, almost everyone raises her hand! The girls are excited because growing up means having more opportunities to do things on their own, but they are nervous about whether they will be ready for it. They also wonder what it will be like to have their bodies change so much. Sometimes they are embarrassed or even a little scared to ask about the changes they will go through on the way to becoming women.

The mothers I talk to are excited to watch their daughters grow up, and they want to see them succeed and be happy. But they've been through the physical and emotional changes of growing up. They know the happy and sad parts of having girlfriends and friends that are boys—and later, the thrills and pains of first romance. They know it can be confusing and difficult at times. And they know their daughters will have to deal with many things on their own because mothers can't be around every minute. But even when their daughters are on their own, mothers still care and want to help. And being helpful isn't always easy for mothers. Just like their daughters, they don't always know how to bring up the topics their daughters need to know about.

Daughters, think of the ways you have already grown up. You've done a lot more than just getting taller each year! Think of the responsibilities you have now that you didn't have a few years ago. You have a lot more homework, and it's harder than it used to be. You call friends, plan overnights, and join clubs. Maybe you do dishes or even cook. Maybe you stay home by yourself some of the time, or look after your little brother or sister. You do many more things on your own than you used to. Every year you spend more time doing things that involve your parents less. Your mother finds it harder and harder to keep up with your life. She doesn't always know what is happening in your world away from home.

I am not suggesting that mothers and daughters tell each other *everything*. That would be a *long* conversation! You have to decide what information you want from each other and what issues you need help with. I am also not suggesting that daughters should avoid making decisions on their own. After all, that's what growing up is all about—learning to make decisions. I am suggesting that mothers and daughters remember that talking to each other can be a big help. It can make the adolescent years a lot happier.

How Well Do You Know Each Other?

OKAY, SO YOU'VE lived together forever and you think you know each other. People who live together for a long time get used to each other. They are busy keeping up with the tasks of daily life, such as getting to school or work or activities on time, with the right papers or uniforms or equipment. They don't ask a lot about each other because they get caught up in their own lives. They think they know each other because they are together so much, and they don't pay attention to details. For instance, sometimes we learn something about another person, store that information away, and assume, even months or years later, that it's still true. When something changes, we just don't notice right away. That's why it sometimes surprises mothers when they look closely one day and their little girl isn't so little anymore.

On the next page is an exercise to see how well you know each other. It is a fun test of whether you have been paying attention to each other.

If you are like most mothers and daughters, you will not get all the answers right about the other person. You probably won't know a few of these simple facts about the person you have lived with for years! Most likely there are other important things you can learn about that person, such as how she feels about friends, household rules, or growing up.

Same, but Different

DAUGHTERS, SOME of the changes that happen during the adolescent years may already be happening to you. You may be growing taller very fast or your feet may seem too big. You may already be developing breasts. Maybe your energy level changes a lot from one hour to the next, from hyperdrive to slow motion and back again. Maybe your moods change quickly from super-happy to tears. We will be talking about these changes and many others in later chapters. But first you need to know that the very same changes happen to every girl, no matter when she grows up. Your mother and grandmother went through these changes, too.

Of course, depending on when you live your life, these

MOTHERS AND DAUGHTERS:

Number a paper from 1 to 10, just like in school, but you don't get graded on this one. There are no right or wrong answers. Make two columns. In the first column, list the following information about yourself:

1. My favorite food
2. My favorite color
3. My best friend at this time
4. Something I always seem to say
5. My favorite TV show
6. My favorite holiday
7. My favorite sport
8. My favorite candy
9. My favorite family activity
10. What I'm really good at doing

In the column next to your answers about yourself, write what you think the other person will say about herself. What is *her* favorite color, and so forth?

Compare your answers. Did she say what you thought she would say about herself? Was she right about your answers? Did you learn something new?

changes happen under very different circumstances. For instance, in the not too distant past, family life was not the way it is today. Most women didn't work outside their homes. People didn't move around as much for school and jobs, and many of them lived all their lives in the town where they were born. Many never used day care or even a baby-sitter. And divorce was rare.

Years ago, the unwritten rules about how women or girls were supposed to behave were different, too. When your grandmother was young, girls weren't allowed to be involved in most organized sports. They were supposed to wear dresses, not pants. Most of them didn't grow up to have careers. And women were not expected to want or need to go to college. Books like this one weren't around, and girls rarely had the kind of talks about growing up your mother will have with you. Women simply didn't talk about the changes in their bodies that we will discuss, sometimes even with their doctors. My grandmother never even saw a doctor until she delivered her first baby!

Society also was very different when your mother was a girl. Children were not exposed to alcohol, drugs, and crime as early as they are today. Suggestions to do things that aren't good for you weren't as common on the radio, in movies, and in magazines. In fact, your mother may have grown up without cable or color television (or even any television at all)! Kids today see and hear a lot of things much earlier in their lives than their parents did.

No wonder everyone's just a little nervous about this growing-up stuff. Making the right decisions was hard even when times were simpler and girls didn't face as many decisions until an older age. These days it can be very confusing.

Just for the record, teenagers today sometimes get a bad rap because people talk so much about the ones who skip class or do drugs or steal cars. But most teenagers are responsible. And most of the time they make good decisions about how to behave.

Grown-ups sometimes get a bad rap, too. Because things were different when your mother was younger, people sometimes talk about a generation gap. They think mothers couldn't possibly understand how things are now because they were not the same back then. Don't make the mistake of thinking that your mother doesn't understand the

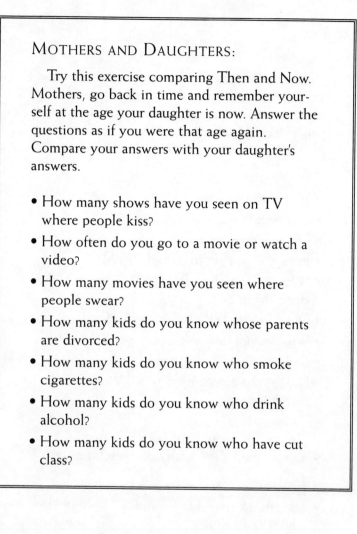

MOTHERS AND DAUGHTERS:

Try this exercise comparing Then and Now. Mothers, go back in time and remember yourself at the age your daughter is now. Answer the questions as if you were that age again. Compare your answers with your daughter's answers.

- How many shows have you seen on TV where people kiss?
- How often do you go to a movie or watch a video?
- How many movies have you seen where people swear?
- How many kids do you know whose parents are divorced?
- How many kids do you know who smoke cigarettes?
- How many kids do you know who drink alcohol?
- How many kids do you know who have cut class?

pressure that is out there—drugs, alcohol, and crime, to name a few. Remember, she's living in this world, too. She listens to the news, goes to work, and talks to friends. She knows. She had to make decisions about the same things at some point in her life, too, maybe just not as young as you will. She also experienced a body that changed, friends who liked her one day and not the next, and disagreements with her parents. She had to figure out what she wanted to do

DAUGHTERS:

Practice getting your mother to answer a few more questions. (After you hear her talking about what growing up was like for her, you might feel like talking more about yourself, too.)

Ask your mother, "When you were my age . . ."

- Where did you live?
- Did your family live in a house?
- Did you ever get lonely?
- How did you get to school?
- Who was your best friend? How far away did she or he live?
- Did you ever feel like no one understood you?
- What lessons (like dance or music) did you take?
- Did you ever have a friend stop liking you?
- Did you have a computer? A TV? A phone? A calculator?

To get a sense of your family's history, ask your mother if she has any of the following:

- A picture of her at your age
- A yearbook from her junior high or high school
- A photo of her and your dad before you were around
- A genealogy, or family tree, listing relatives as far back as they have been traced
- Some music or stories from your family's ethnic group

with her life and how to do it. She knows what it is like to grow up.

What your mother doesn't always know is what is going on in your life away from home—in school and with your friends. If something isn't going well, she might hear about it from a teacher or another parent. But she won't know how to help unless she knows what is happening to you, and what you think and feel about it. And she won't know that unless you tell her.

What Do You Want from Her?

IT'S EASY TO THINK we know what somebody else thinks or feels. But as we found out earlier, it's also easy to be wrong. Since I can't ask you questions directly, I can't know how you feel about things. But I can tell you what a lot of mothers and daughters say *they* feel. You will have to tell each other which of the feelings fit in your situation. First, most mothers and daughters want to stay friends with each other. Not just friends in the sense of having a good time together, but friends who trust each other, talk, share feelings, and work through problems as they come up. Mothers and daughters want to face adolescence—and the rest of life—as a team. Second, they both want the daughter to feel good about herself and have fun along the way to building her future.

Despite having similar goals, mothers and daughters have different needs as the daughter grows up. For instance, mothers have taken care of their daughters for a long time and want to make sure they stay safe. If I put together the things mothers tell me they feel about their daughters growing up, it would go something like this:

> *My goal is to keep my daughter safe while letting her go a little at a time. I trust her more than*

*she thinks, and I want her to do things on her own.
It's just that I know there are dangers out there.
Sometimes when kids get together in groups, they
make decisions that no one child would make by
herself; they perform more daring, dangerous acts
and are less concerned about what might happen.
This is probably because they don't stop to think
about their actions, or maybe because no one wants
to look like she's chicken or a spoilsport. I want so
much to know that my daughter can stand up to
that sort of pressure and make the right choices. But
I know it is very hard and that no one does it 100
percent of the time. I just want her to know I'm on
her side and want to help. I'm not the enemy here!*

The girls I talk to have been pretty carefree to this point
and naturally want to stay that way. It's just that the meaning
of the word *carefree* changes as they get older. Daughters
don't need their mothers to do as many things for them as
they once did, and they want to be more independent. They
want to fill their lives with fun new experiences and friends.
They know that having freedom means taking on more
responsibility, and they are anxious to show their mothers
they can handle more freedom.

Even though there are good intentions on both sides,
the needs of mothers and daughters sometimes clash. *Be safe*
and *Learn responsibility* comes across as "You can't handle it"
or "I don't trust you," and *Give me some freedom* and *I want
to have fun* comes across as "I don't care about you or your
rules." Then angry words and hostile behavior hide what was
really meant. A mother might need to be convinced that a situation is safe or that her daughter can stand up to peer pressure. When a mother makes rules or sets consequences, she
really is saying that she cares about her daughter.

MOTHERS AND DAUGHTERS:

Here are some feelings mothers and daughters tell me they have. You may or may not feel the same way. Go through the list and say whether you ever have the feelings described.

Mothers often say:

- I want to be sure my daughter is safe.
- I need to be able to trust my daughter to do what she promises.
- I need my daughter to know that when I say no or get irritated, I still love her.
- I want to be thanked sometimes for the things I do.
- I need to do some things just for myself once in a while.
- I need hugs.
- I need my daughter to know that I am on her side.
- I need to know what is going on in my daughter's life.
- I want to know my daughter still needs me.
- I need to have my daughter's grown-up, responsible behaviors pointed out to me when I am not paying attention to them.

Daughters often say:

- I want to be told I am doing a good job even if it is obvious.
- I need to know I am important to my mother.
- I need to know my mother is proud of me.
- I want to be told I did something in a responsible way.
- I need to be told my mother wants me to grow up, not to hold me back.
- I need to know my mother loves me even when she dislikes the way I'm acting.
- I want to be given the chance to show my mother I can handle myself.
- I need some privacy—a space (even a drawer) that is mine that the family won't rummage through.
- I need to be told "I love you" even when I'm moody.
- I need hugs.

A daughter is just being a normal preteen when she pushes for more independence. But sometimes the answer to a request is no. Then she may need to be reminded that often it is the possible dangers, not her behavior, that cause parents to draw the line. It might help a mother to hear that her daughter has thought about how she will handle herself. It might help a daughter to hear that if the situation had been just a little different, the answer might be yes. Sometimes mothers and daughters need to hear things from each other that just don't get said. When these clashes happen, talking together—just like you'll be doing in all the exercises in this book—helps you understand what the other person feels, even though you won't always agree.

CHAPTER 2

How to Talk to Each Other

Why Some Conversations Never Have a Chance

CONVERSATIONS OFTEN start out like quizzes. Someone tries to get information from someone else by asking questions. Sometimes that works great. But a true/false quiz, one that asks whether something is true or not, doesn't require a long answer. "Did you have a good day at school?" asks for only a yes or a no, and doesn't often get more. If you want to know what happened at school, you might have to ask an essay question—one that asks for an explanation. Like "How was your day?" or even more specifically, "What happened at school today?" Usually this will lead to sharing more about what's important to both people.

But did you ever have a conversation like this one?

Mom:	How was school today?
Daughter:	Fine.
Mom:	What did you do?
Daughter:	Nothing.
Mom:	What did you learn?

Daughter:	I dunno.
Mom:	Where are you going?
Daughter:	Nowhere.

Or one like this?

Daughter:	How was work?
Mom:	Busy.
Daughter:	What happened?
Mom:	Nothing new.
Daughter:	What are we doing tonight?
Mom:	I dunno.

These are the shortest essays I've ever seen! You don't learn much about the other person's life with a conversation like that! You may really want to talk, but if you continue shooting questions at the other person, she may feel she is being grilled. And you may think she just doesn't want to share her experiences with you.

Why didn't these "quizzes" get the answers the mother or daughter hoped for? A conversation may never get off the ground for a lot of reasons—such as when it happens, where it happens, who is being asked to talk, and how the other person reacts. Let's talk about some of these reasons.

The Wrong Time to Talk

SOMETIMES OTHER people don't seem to listen when we try to talk to them. Our questions don't seem important to them or appear to annoy them. We think they don't care and feel angry about being ignored. Maybe the real problem is just that it is the wrong time to try to talk.

Here is a list of the ten *worst* times to start a conversation that is important to you:

- When the other person is trying to tell *you* something
- When she is already talking to someone else
- When she is on the phone
- When either of you is in a big hurry
- When you are so angry you might say something unkind
- When you are both tired and cranky
- When people you don't want to listen are around
- When the other person isn't taking you seriously
- When you are continually interrupted by other people or things
- When there is a lot of noise in the room

Meaningful communication *can* happen at these times, but it is much less likely when you don't have the other person's full attention. Sometimes it is best to wait and hold the conversation at some other time or place. Here are some times that might be easier to talk to each other:

During a Meal. Mealtime offers a great opportunity to talk to other family members and find out how things are going for them. Families that eat at least a few meals together each week tend to feel more connected to each other and to know each other better. This is a good time to ask essay questions about others' lives. If such questions don't get people talking, here's another way to start the conversation. Actually, it's more like a sentence completion quiz.

At our house, we sometimes take turns starting a sentence to which everyone else gives an ending, one at a time. Sometimes we are silly, but most of the time we say what's on our mind. We start sentences like "What I liked about today was ... " or "The worst part about today was ... "

MOTHERS AND DAUGHTERS:

Try completing these sentences yourselves. Take turns being the first one to finish each sentence, but make sure you both give an answer. Then think of other beginnings of sentences that might be fun to finish.

The best thing about today was _____
_____.

I like _____
_____.

Today I found out _____
_____.

I laughed today when _____
_____.

The thing I liked least about today was _____
_____.

I felt angry when _____
_____.

I wish _____
_____.

Tomorrow I hope to _____
_____.

I was embarrassed when _____
_____.

I remember _____
_____.

We get a lot of interesting comments that really get us talking.

Conversations over meals don't have to happen just at dinnertime. Breakfast and lunch are fair game, too. A conversation that needs to be private might have to take place at a meal for two, just you and your mother.

At Bedtime. Somehow bedtime brings the talk out of people. Not just "Can I have a drink?" or "Where's my pillow?" but real conversation. Maybe it's because you are in the dark and don't look directly at each other. Maybe it's because the tasks of the day are behind you and you can relax a little. Or maybe you just don't want to go to sleep! Whatever the reason, starting a conversation at bedtime can be great. Occasionally making bedtime just a little earlier can provide more time if you really need to talk.

One word of caution here. Sometimes people get more emotional when they are tired; even little problems seem like big ones. Tears start, and something that really needs to be discussed doesn't get finished. If this happens, remember that (as my mother often said) things will look better in the morning, and save the rest of the conversation for then. A back rub or a hug may be all that is needed to keep someone from going to sleep very sad or worried. Just make sure that the subject one of you wanted to discuss does not get forgotten in the light of day.

Riding in the Car. Driving in the car often gets conversations going. This is especially true when just two people are in the car, the radio is off, and the drive takes more than fifteen minutes. Again, not facing each other directly may be one of the reasons it's easier to talk in this situation. Or maybe it's just because neither party can escape! Don't forget that you can park the car somewhere for a while if you need more time.

While Doing a Simple Activity Together. Conversations often start when people do an activity together. They seem to relax and enjoy themselves. It can be fun to talk while baking cookies, riding a bicycle (if you don't get too out of breath!), or doing a jigsaw puzzle. Any activity that doesn't involve a lot of thinking can offer a great opportunity for conversation, though I have to admit I once left the eggs out of a cake this way!

Here is a list of activities the two of you may want to try. Even if they don't start you talking, you will enjoy spending the time together anyway!

- Playing checkers
- Drawing pictures
- Fishing
- Sculpting with clay
- Swinging
- Walking around the block
- Having a picnic lunch in the backyard
- Curling hair
- Painting fingernails or toenails
- Grooming the dog
- Playing with the cat
- Sewing
- Carpentry
- Painting the house
- Fixing something that is broken
- Cooking or baking

You *Never Talk and You Want* Her *To?*

Having a really good conversation takes two. And it is definitely easier for some people to talk than others. We all know someone who could ramble on forever about any subject,

MOTHERS AND DAUGHTERS:

Pick one of these topics for the other person to talk about for thirty seconds. Time her. She doesn't have to say anything important, just talk about the topic—anything she can think of to say. Here are some helpful hints: What does it look like? How do you know that? What experience have you had with it? And so on. Anything is fair game; the goal is just to keep talking. Feel free to come up with your own topics, too.

Crayons	Mermaids
Shoelaces	Car engines
Snare drums	Math class
Cantaloupes	Spaceships
Candles	Silly Putty or Gak™
Erasers	Outhouses

someone to whom you could say, "Talk for ten minutes about how you feel about rain," and she could do it, no problem. But for some people, talking is not so easy, and discussing feelings is really difficult.

How did you do with this exercise? It may have been easy or difficult for you to talk about something for that amount of time. Either way, you may find it harder to talk about your feelings about things than to just rattle off facts. This is especially true when your feelings about something are strong. For example, it is easier to say that someone called you a name than to admit that this act hurt your feelings or you'd like an apology. It is easier to talk about someone's not doing what she promised than to say you are angry.

How we talk about feelings is often learned by watching others do it, and a girl often learns her mother's ways of saying what she wants or needs or feels. By observing what her mother says and does, she gets a pretty good sense of how her mother feels about herself, what she thinks about others, and how she solves problems.

As a daughter, you have probably watched your mother laugh, cry, and get angry at different times in her life. If she does not talk much during these situations, you are left having to guess what she is thinking or feeling. This information is a lot more important than her favorite color or candy! You might think, "Was she angry when she said that?" or "Does she think he is smarter than her?" or "Was she disappointed when she didn't get that done?" If you wonder about the answers, you might want to ask some questions. You might understand your mother's feelings better if you ask her to do some of her thinking out loud now and then. Having her say what she thinks or feels can clear up wrong ideas and start some interesting conversation.

Now, I know what you mothers are going to say. Talking to yourself out loud can feel very strange (and you probably don't want to do it just anywhere!). But think seriously about what your daughter watches you do each day. She sees you work, take care of the house, and manage the kids. She watches you organize activities and handle relationships. She knows she may be doing many of these things herself someday. Even if you are always calm and collected (and who is?), what you handle in the course of day can look pretty overwhelming. You may leave her guessing what you are thinking or feeling—and how you handle the stress.

As a mother you solve a lot of problems every day without saying a word about them. But if you talk out loud about situations while they are happening, your daughter will have a better chance of figuring out how you do it. For example, one mother's speech went something like this:

> *Let's see, I need to get some cash, put gas in the car, buy milk for breakfast, and pick your father up by five. He needs to get home by five-thirty, and it's a twenty-minute drive. I'm so frustrated. I'm not going to get everything done! I'd better put gas in the car or we won't get home at all. I'm angry at myself for not doing that earlier, but I can still get a few things done. I'll pick up your dad, see if he has any cash, take him home, and go out for milk later. If he needs the car, maybe he can get the milk, or maybe we'll just have eggs for breakfast. I'd rather get it all done, but I'm okay with this solution.*

If you can't talk about decisions while you are making them, it can still be helpful to explain them later. Do the exercise on page 32 to practice talking about problem situations, feelings, and solutions all at once. Take turns giving your answers. Be sure not to talk about family finances or marital relationships. These are adult-to-adult topics, and not things daughters should have to be concerned with.

Practice this exercise once in a while to get used to talking about your experiences and your feelings. If one of you is having a particularly difficult time talking about herself, here's a way for the other person to help. When you want someone to feel more comfortable talking to you, show her what you mean. Sit on the other person's bed a few nights and start talking. Talk for ten minutes about yourself—again, not about adult issues such as money or husbands, but about what happened during your day, how you

MOTHERS AND DAUGHTERS:

Think about a difficult situation you dealt with recently, a time when you needed to get several things done but had to pick the most important one to start. Talk about it by finishing the following sentences:

I had all these things to get done: _____

_____.

I felt _____.

I could have _____.

But I chose to _____

    because_____.

The result was_____.

Then I felt_____.

solved problems, and how you feel about things. Then stop and ask her how her day was. If you get a brief response or no response at all, let it be. Don't say anything critical. Do the same thing night after night, accepting if the other person doesn't want to talk. By the third or fourth night, the other person will be so tired of hearing you talk, she might just talk about herself! And you will have shown her how to do it.

How Will She React?

TALKING TO SOMEONE can be difficult if you are concerned about what she will say or do in response. You may worry she will think you are silly, pushy, or rude. If a response seems too quick or thoughtless, you may feel laughed at or judged, then hurt or angry, and you may stop trying to talk. No topic should be taboo. Mothers and daughters need to feel free to bring up any subject. That doesn't mean, of course, that every personal question will or should be answered. Certainly there are some adult issues that should not be discussed in detail. But overreacting to a question or an answer can stop a conversation short. If you know the other person won't get angry, think you are foolish, or try to solve the problem with a lecture, it is easier to talk.

I remember the night I was putting one of my daughters to bed. (She was younger at the time than you are.) I was rubbing her back and asked her how she liked her new bus driver. She mumbled, "Fine, except when she goes to sleep." Of course my immediate urge was to grab her and holler, "*What?*" That would have convinced her she had said something wrong and have started her crying, and I might not have heard the rest of the story. Fortunately, I kept rubbing her back and calmly said, "Oh? When did that happen?" She told me the driver nodded off at a stop sign because she worked two jobs and was tired. Needless to say, she never rode with that driver again!

To help you avoid responses that can shut down an important conversation, here are a few suggestions:

- Don't act shocked at anything that comes up.
  You will get more information if you simply say,
  "That surprises me. Tell me more about it."
- Don't overreact by saying things like "You've
  got to be kidding!" or "That's ridiculous!"
- Listen to what the other person has to say.
  Don't offer advice too fast.
- Be patient while the other person speaks.
  Assume you don't know what she will say.

- Ask what the speaker thinks she should do about the problem.
- Don't gloat if the situation turned out just like you said it would. "I told you so" hardly ever needs to be pointed out.
- If you need more information, ask for it.
- Never laugh or tease about something the other person wants you to take seriously.
- Talk about the issue again later if you need to.

How to Start a Difficult Conversation

SOMETIMES MOTHERS and daughters just don't know how to bring up a topic. For instance, one girl told me she was concerned about her breast development. She said she wanted to talk to me instead of her mother because she was afraid her mother would laugh. She said she liked to talk to her mother while riding in their car, but she just couldn't cruise along staring at the trees and then suddenly throw in: "Do you know why one of my breasts is bigger than the other?" She needed a more natural way to start the conversation.

Some of the hardest conversations for anyone to start are these:

- When you are a little (or a lot!) embarrassed but need the information
- When you've been told the answer before but are hoping for a different one
- When you have sad news
- When you want something but don't think the other person is going to agree
- When the other person might get emotional— angry or sad or embarrassed—about the topic

MOTHERS AND DAUGHTERS:

Each of you think about the last time you brought up a difficult topic to the other person. Here are some topics you might have found hard to talk about:

- Homework
- Grades
- Rules
- Changes in your body
- Friends
- Teachers
- An argument
- Brothers or sisters

Name two things the other person did that made it easier for you to talk. Here are some possibilities:

- She listened.
- She gave me the information I needed.
- She asked my opinion.
- She waited to be asked for her opinion.
- She brought the subject up again later.
- She suggested we talk when the timing was better.
- She didn't say, "I told you so."
- She didn't criticize me.
- She asked me for more information.
- She told me about something similar that happened to her.

If you have difficulty bringing up a subject you really want to talk about, here is a four-step plan that may make it easier:

1. *Ask to talk.* Make sure the other person knows you want to talk and is able to listen at the time. If the time isn't right, a lot of uh-huhs get said without one person's paying full attention to the other. Ask:

- "Can we talk?"
- "Do you have time to listen to me now? I need to talk to you."
- "Is this a good time to ask you something?"

2. *Say that you have been thinking about something.*

"I've been thinking about what you said yesterday."
"I've been thinking about something that happened at school today."
"I've been thinking about some things in that book about growing up."

3. *If you are uncomfortable, afraid of the response, or embarrassed, say so.*

"This is kind of embarrassing, so please don't laugh."
"I'm not sure you'll agree, so just listen, okay?"
"I know you gave me your answer before, but can we discuss this some more?"

4. *Take a deep breath and say it.*

"Why is one of my breasts bigger than the other?"
"Can I go to Sara's party?"
"I have a problem with my math grade."

When Can You Talk Again?

EVERY GOOD conversation deserves another—and makes the next one easier to have! Of course if you feel that the situation is resolved, you don't have to discuss that particular thing again. But if you have further thoughts or feelings after you have finished talking, you might want to bring up the topic again.

Even if you don't need to have another conversation about the same thing, it might feel good just to talk again. To make sure that happens, you may need to let the other person know you would like to talk some more. But when you are busy, talk doesn't just happen. So here are a few suggestions:

- Use the steps just described and say, "I've been thinking how nice it was to talk the other day."
- Write a note to the other person that says, "I'd like to talk again."
- Plan when to have the next talk before you end the one you are having.
- Pick a date on the calendar, and decide what you will do (if anything) while you talk.
- Make a regular appointment, like every other Saturday at lunch.
- Use a message board and write: "I need to talk!"
- Ask at bedtime, "Do you want to read or just talk?"
- Leave a silly reminder on the other's pillow. (One girl chose a set of wind-up teeth; another, a pair of candy lips!)

There's no doubt about it, talking with each other can open the door to a lot of interesting subjects. But when you are busy, talk doesn't just happen. Someone has to start, and the other has to listen and respond with caring and attention. Once you have made it that far, you will find that mothers and daughters can discuss just about anything.

CHAPTER 3

How Girls' Bodies Change

DAUGHTERS, YOU KNOW that your body will be changing over
the next few years. You may have seen videos, read books,
or talked to your friends about growing up. Most girls feel
a mixture of excitement, nervousness, pride, and confusion
about what is ahead. They often want to talk to their mothers
about what they can expect but at the same time feel a little
shy or embarrassed. I hope that reading this chapter together
will help both of you feel comfortable discussing what it is
like to grow up.

Mothers, you may remember the changes your body
went through as you gradually went from having a girl's body
to having the shape of a grown-up woman. You probably had
some mixed feelings, too, as you went through those changes.

Signs of Puberty

YOUR MOTHER probably remembers a time when she grew
taller very quickly, a time when relatives started saying things
like "My, how you've grown!" and "Isn't she long-legged?"

DAUGHTERS:

Ask your mother:

- What was the first change you noticed in your body that told you you were growing up?
- How old were you?
- What feelings did you have about it?
- Who did you talk with about it?

She probably was beginning her growth spurt, which signaled that puberty was on the way. Puberty is the name for the time in a young girl's life when her body begins to change into a more adult form.

Your growth spurt will likely begin somewhere around age eleven, but it could easily start at any point between nine and thirteen years of age. Over the course of a few months to a year and a half, your body will grow more quickly than it has since you were a baby. Your clothing will quickly get too small. This period of growth will begin with changes in your hands, legs, and feet, and for a time, they may seem too large for the rest of your body. Because your body will be changing so quickly, you may feel clumsy now and again. This will improve as time goes on. You may also find that you are very hungry and need more sleep than usual. Growing takes energy, and energy comes from eating the right food and getting enough rest. Don't worry; as your body catches up to itself over the next year or so, your need for food and sleep will lessen, too. Just relax and follow your body's signals.

About the time you begin your growth spurt, you will probably notice other changes of puberty. The most obvious will be that your breasts will begin to grow. You will also notice hair beginning to grow in the area over your pubic bone (the bone that is several inches below your navel). Later, you will have your first period. You may already have started having periods, or you may not even know what they are yet. In any case, keep reading. You will learn answers to some of your questions and think of others to ask your mother. Puberty is a time of some pretty exciting changes. Talking about them is a great way to understand what is happening and get ready for the changes still to come.

The changes of puberty will begin when your body is ready. When it is time, a gland in your brain will start producing a chemical (or hormone) that signals the body to begin to mature. The changes will not happen all at once; your body will take years to reach the form it will have when you are a woman. Your friends may be ahead of you or behind you in the process. None of the changes happen to everyone at exactly the same age or in exactly the same way. You may end up having large breasts or small ones. You may start your period before or after your friends. And you may end up taller or shorter than they are. If you are small now compared with your friends, you will probably be small compared with them when you are finished growing. And if you are one of the taller girls, you will probably stay taller when you are older. But height, like breast size, doesn't make you better or worse than anyone else. I was the smallest in my class (probably on both counts) and it didn't make any major difference in my life, except for dodging people's elbows and being put in the front row of every photograph. And don't worry if you are taller than the boys. They will catch up. Their growth spurt starts a couple of years later than it does for girls.

One thing you can be pretty sure of is that the changes you will go through will happen in about the same order

MOTHERS AND DAUGHTERS:

One of the signs that girls are heading
for puberty is that they talk more to each other
about their bodies than they did when they
were younger. There are a lot of expressions
and slang words for the parts that change most,
like *boobs* and *tits*. Name a few others you can
think of right now. In the weeks to come, discuss them together when you hear them. Girls,
if you hear any you don't recognize, ask your
mother to help you understand. If you haven't
discussed it already, ask her which ones she
thinks are okay to say to other people.

they do for everyone else. These changes happen in a
series of stages. Girls go through several stages before their
bodies look like a woman's body. You will be able to figure
out what stage you are in now as you read the next few
pages.

Breast Development

YOUR BREASTS will begin to change when you are anywhere
from eight to thirteen years old, but most girls don't notice
much change until they are around age eleven. The first thing
you will probably notice is that the area under the nipple
begins to grow into a little mound, raising the nipple up slightly.
These breast buds are one of the earliest signs of puberty.

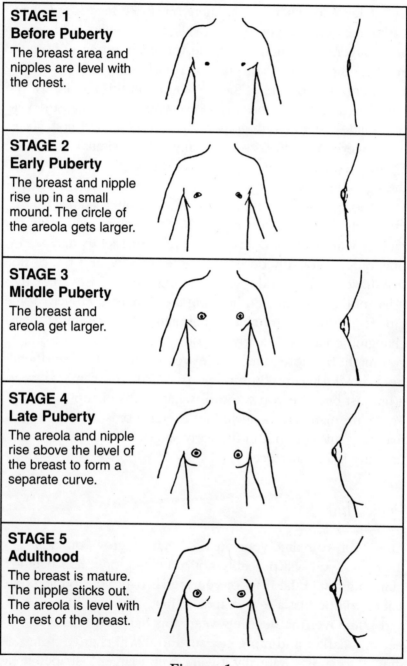

STAGE 1
Before Puberty

The breast area and nipples are level with the chest.

STAGE 2
Early Puberty

The breast and nipple rise up in a small mound. The circle of the areola gets larger.

STAGE 3
Middle Puberty

The breast and areola get larger.

STAGE 4
Late Puberty

The areola and nipple rise above the level of the breast to form a separate curve.

STAGE 5
Adulthood

The breast is mature. The nipple sticks out. The areola is level with the rest of the breast.

Figure 1

A few months to a year after you notice breast buds, the darker area around your nipple, called the areola, will begin to grow larger. Even later, the nipple will push out away from the areola and the rest of your breast. Your breasts may be a little sore from time to time as they develop, but this almost always improves as puberty goes on. Don't worry if one breast develops a little faster than the other. This is normal and not cause for concern. Your breasts eventually will be similar in size. Figure 1 contains some drawings of the stages you will go through. See if you can identify the one you are in right now.

The question of when to wear a bra often comes up even before breast buds appear. It is something you and your mother will want to discuss. Some of your friends may wear one; others probably do not. Whether they wear a bra or not may have nothing to do with how big their breasts are. (And it has nothing to do with how big their breasts will get.) Some girls feel more comfortable if their shirts do not outline their changing breasts so clearly. If your breasts are a little sore, you might be more comfortable wearing a bra to keep them from moving when you run and play. But you can also wear a bra just because you want to. What you do is up to you. There are many styles, including exercise bras and half tops, that may suit you, but in the early stages of puberty you may find any bra a nuisance.

Pubic Hair

ABOUT THE SAME time your breasts begin to grow, or soon thereafter, you will probably notice light-colored hair beginning to grow in the front of your pelvis over your pubic bone. There will be just a few strands at first, and they will be soft and fine. Over the next few years this hair will gradually become darker and more coarse, and it will change from straight to curly. Gradually it will cover a larger V-shaped area

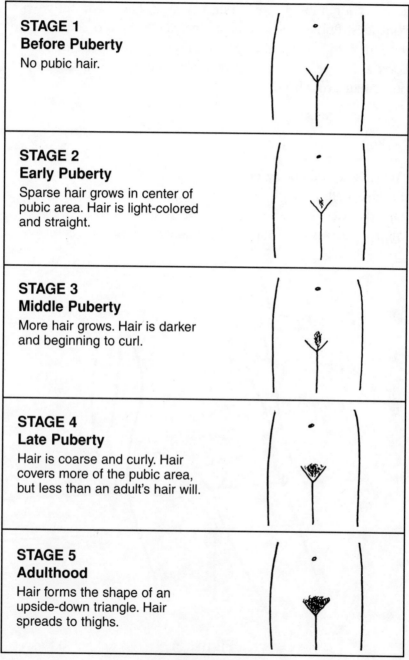

STAGE 1
Before Puberty
No pubic hair.

STAGE 2
Early Puberty
Sparse hair grows in center of pubic area. Hair is light-colored and straight.

STAGE 3
Middle Puberty
More hair grows. Hair is darker and beginning to curl.

STAGE 4
Late Puberty
Hair is coarse and curly. Hair covers more of the pubic area, but less than an adult's hair will.

STAGE 5
Adulthood
Hair forms the shape of an upside-down triangle. Hair spreads to thighs.

Figure 2

across your pubic bone. Later, it will extend back between your legs. Pubic hair is almost always curlier and coarser than the hair on your head, and it usually ends up being darker. Look at Figure 2 and see if you can identify which stage of pubic hair growth you are in now.

Periods

THE REASON your body begins to mature during puberty is that it is getting ready to be an adult, an adult who will someday decide if she wants to become a mother. Every animal has a way of having babies. And their babies grow

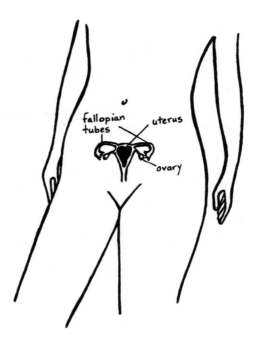

Figure 3

up to have babies of their own. That is how nature makes sure that each type of animal continues to exist. Your body already has the parts it will need as an adult, but it has to go through puberty for those parts to develop and be ready to have children.

Being female, you were born with an area inside your body where a baby could someday grow. This area, called the uterus (or womb), is not the same thing as your stomach, even though women sometimes say they have a baby in their "tummy." It is a separate place about the size and shape of a pear, and men and boys do not have one (see Figure 3). Once a month an egg comes into the uterus from another part of your body called the ovaries. (Males don't have these, either.) The ovaries are two tiny areas, each about the size of a plum, that are located on either side of the uterus. Each ovary has many cells inside that could eventually grow into babies if they join with a man's sperm cell, but they are not ready to do that. When you reach puberty, one egg matures each month in one ovary or the other. When it is ready, the egg is pushed from the ovary. This is called ovulation. That egg, which is too small to be seen without a microscope, moves down a tube (called a fallopian tube) to your uterus.

Each month, the uterus gets ready to receive an egg by becoming soft and lined with blood. If a baby were going to grow there, it would need the nutrients and oxygen in the blood in order to develop. Since you won't be growing a baby at this point in your life, the blood that builds up during each month will not be needed. It will break up after a week or so and flow out of the uterus through the vagina. The vagina is the opening between your legs right behind your urethra (where urine comes out). When this blood flows out of your vagina, you will be having a period. The real name for it is menstruation, but most people call it a period.

Periods happen about every twenty-eight days, and they last from three to seven days.

When Will You Start Having Periods?

It is hard to say when you will start having periods. You may already have begun, or it may be a few years before you do. Remember, you may develop earlier or later than your friends, and that's just fine. We're all a little different. Even though you can't know exactly when you will start, there are some ways to make a good guess about it. Most often, menstruation begins about two years after you notice the first changes of puberty—your growth spurt, breast development, or pubic hair. Most girls begin having periods when they are twelve or thirteen years old, but it is not unusual for them to start anywhere between nine and sixteen years of age.

A girl often has her first period around the same time her mother started hers. If you have an older sister, you will probably start your periods about the same age she did. But other things can affect when your periods start. You must have good nutrition to have periods. If you are too thin or have poor nutrition due to an illness or dieting, your periods could be delayed or not come at all.

What Is It Like to Have a Period?

You will probably know when you have your first period, but you should talk to your mother about any discharge that comes from your vagina. A period usually starts as a red or brown spot of blood in your underclothes, but you may have

DAUGHTERS:

Ask your mother these questions and any others you can think of:

• How old were you when you started menstruating (having periods)?

• Where were you?

• Did you know about periods ahead of time?

• How did you find out?

signs before then that your body is getting ready to start. You may have a clear discharge from your vagina for several months before your period starts. Red, brown, and clear colors are normal. A yellowish or smelly discharge, though, can be a sign of infection. Tell your mother about it right away. Most infections are easily treated by a doctor.

The blood during a period flows out by itself and is not something you can control. The bleeding itself does not hurt. However, because the uterus is shedding its lining, you may have some cramps before or during your period. Cramps are usually not painful and disappear after a few days, but some girls feel very uncomfortable when they have cramps. If you do, tell your mother. You can try putting a hot water bottle or heating pad on your abdomen, and some medications you can buy without a prescription work well to relieve cramps. If these things don't help, talk to your doctor. There is no need to suffer.

Taking Care of Yourself

TAKING CARE OF yourself during your period is a lot easier today than it used to be. There are many convenient products available to keep the blood from getting on your clothes. One such product is called a feminine napkin. It is an absorbent pad that has one sticky side for attaching it to the inside of your underwear. Napkins come in different sizes. When blood is flowing the most during your period, you will want to wear a thick one, or one called a maxipad. Toward the end of your period, when the flow is no more than a spot now and then, you might want to wear a thinner one. Thin pads are sometimes called panty liners.

MOTHERS:

- Tell about the feminine napkins you first had when you were a girl.

- Were they different in size from the ones you can buy today?

- How did they fasten?

Today, feminine napkins are simple to use, and other people can't tell when you are wearing them. But they need to be changed every four to six hours. Blood does not have much odor by itself, but it can smell bad when it comes in contact with the bacteria on your skin. Keep the area around your vagina clean and change the pad several times a day.

DAUGHTERS:

- Ask your mother to show you a feminine napkin and a tampon.

- Ask her to show you where she keeps them.

- Ask her if there are other types or sizes she thinks would be better for you.

- Ask her for some supplies of your own that you can keep on hand.

Some women find feminine napkins bulky and uncomfortable and don't like that they can't be worn in a bathtub or a pool. There is a simple product that solves these problems—the tampon. The tampon was designed to let women do all their normal activities, including swimming,

DAUGHTERS:

- Ask your mother how you should get rid of used napkins or tampons at home.

- Ask her what she thinks you should do if you start at school, like having a supply of napkins on hand or making a trip to the nurse's office.

- Talk about any questions you can think of at this point.

while having their period. It is basically an absorbent roll of cotton or cotton-like material that is worn inside the vagina. It is pushed into the vagina with a finger or with a cardboard or plastic applicator that comes with it. Because it is worn internally, a tampon can be more comfortable and less messy than a napkin.

There is no physical reason you can't wear a tampon as soon as you start menstruating, but tampons are not for everyone. It's really a matter of personal choice. Some girls worry about putting a tampon into their vagina, but a tampon can't get lost inside you. It is easily removed by pulling a string that stays attached to it and hangs outside the vagina. And putting a tampon in or taking it out isn't uncomfortable.

There is one word of caution about tampons, however: They need to be changed frequently. Years ago, doctors found that women who wore tampons had more chance of getting an illness called toxic shock syndrome. They noticed the illness mostly among women who used thick tampons and left them in for a long time. But toxic shock syndrome should not be a problem for women who change their tampons frequently, at least every four hours. It is a good idea to wear the smallest size tampon you can for the flow you are having, and to wear a pad at night.

In order for napkins and tampons not to smell bad after they are used, they must be disposed of in the right way. The tampons themselves (but not their applicators) can be flushed down a toilet, but feminine napkins should not be. Toilets can overflow from being clogged this way. Most public rest rooms have a special container in each stall just for throwing away feminine napkins and tampon applicators. At home you may want to put napkins back in their wrappings or wrap them well in toilet tissue before putting them in a trash bag.

Issues of Privacy

THE CHANGES YOUR body goes through during puberty mean that you are on your way to becoming a woman. There will be times when you feel awkward about these changes. After all, you were used to your body looking one way and it is beginning to look different. You may feel grown up one minute and like a little girl the next. Even though you may feel confused or shy at times, the changes in your body are something to be excited about. In earlier times it wasn't considered proper even to talk about such things, but today women are much more open. It is okay to talk to people about growing up, particularly your mother. And you don't need to be embarrassed to ask for a bra or to buy panty liners or tampons in the grocery store. Growing up is a fact of life. Everybody does it.

Sometimes girls tell me they are uncomfortable because their parents talk to each other about the changes they are going through. I remember being embarrassed that my mother told my father I had started shaving my legs (as if he couldn't tell). Many parents see the changes their daughter is going through as rather amazing. They feel proud that she is maturing; it means they succeeded in raising her from a little girl to being a woman. They may even tell their friends or relatives how proud they are. If you are bothered by your parents' openness, tell them how you feel and ask them not to repeat their comments to anyone else.

Little brothers and sisters can be very curious about all this growing-up stuff. They want to listen to your conversations and know everything you are doing, and that can get very irritating. It helps to remember that this annoying behavior probably comes from wanting to be grown up like you. If you really think about it, the fact that he or she wants to be like you is actually a compliment! Often, younger brothers or sisters will stop bugging you if you help them feel more grown up, too. Let them help you with a project, read to them, or teach them about things they haven't learned in school yet. Brothers and sisters can be great friends if you don't let their curiosity get the better of you!

Little brothers and sisters sometimes ask questions about growing up that surprise you or make you uncomfortable. If you don't make a big deal out of it, they will probably take any response you give them pretty matter-of-factly. But be careful not to embarrass them, either. Once when I was little —before I knew about periods—I found a used feminine napkin in a trash can. I asked the adults around if someone had cut herself. I was so embarrassed when they laughed at me! I knew they thought I'd said something funny, but I didn't understand why they were laughing. I thought I had done something wrong. Little brothers and sisters are the same way. They are curious and will ask you questions about things they don't know about. Your best response is probably "It is something older girls need" or "You will learn about this when you are older." If that doesn't stop their questions, suggest that they ask your mother, or ask her what she wants you to tell them.

Sometimes brothers and sisters, older or younger, look for things to tease each other about—including growing up— because they know it bothers the other person. As aggravating as that can be, don't let it make you think that everyone everywhere thinks these things are silly—they don't. Be proud of the fact that you are growing up and remember that brothers and sisters may be teasing because they are jealous that you have more responsibilities and privileges than you used to have—maybe more than they have! Smile, and act like it doesn't bother you. If it really does, though, ask your parents for ideas. Some of the things described in Chapter 9, "Thinking Things Out," can also be helpful when you have a problem with a brother or sister.

Finally, some girls worry that the boys at school will see a napkin or tampon in their purse or backpack. They think they would be so embarrassed they wouldn't be able to go back to school. But when I was in sixth grade I saw an interesting thing happen. A boy found a feminine napkin in a girl's locker. He opened it and tossed it around with his friend, and they all made silly jokes trying to embarrass the girls. But nobody reacted. The girls all looked at him like he was still in kindergarten, and the teacher sent him to the office. It just wasn't worth getting embarrassed about.

CHAPTER 4
Oily Hair, Zits, and Body Odor

EVER SINCE YOU were a little girl you have been told that your body belongs to you. You make it do things you want it to do. You take an interest in the way you dress it. And you are modest about other people looking at it. The closer you get to adulthood, the more responsibility you will have for taking care of your body, and for making sure that no one else pushes you do things that are not good for it. You are at a good age right now to start practicing healthy habits.

Taking Care of Your Skin and Hair

WHEN PUBERTY BEGINS, your brain sends out chemicals called hormones to the rest of your body to start it on its way to becoming a woman. Not only do hormones cause changes in the shape of your body, they affect your skin and hair, too. During puberty, tiny glands in your face, scalp, chest, and back begin to produce oils that come out through the pores in your skin. This can give your skin and hair a shiny, greasy appearance. The increase in oil in your hair is not usually a problem. To keep your hair from looking stringy and dirty, you simply need to wash it each day or every other day. If your hair seems to get dirty very quickly, look for a mild shampoo designed for oily hair.

With your glands giving off more oils, you may notice a few pimples (or acne, or zits, as some people call them) on your face, chest, or back. Pimples can have a raised white or black appearance, or they can be reddish bumps that eventually get a head on them. The reddish ones eventually break open, releasing out a whitish substance called pus. Pimples result when dead skin and oil harden in the oil gland and clogs the opening, or pore. When the pore gets infected and pus pushes into the surrounding skin, redness and swelling result.

Years ago, doctors thought that acne was caused by eating things like chocolate or snack food. Actually, what you eat has little to do with whether you will get pimples or not. Doctors now know that teenage acne runs in families. During your teen years, your skin will probably be similar to the way your parents' skin was as a teenager. If they had acne, you will likely have some pimples too.

MOTHERS:

- Tell whether you had mild, moderate, or severe acne as a teenager.
- How did you feel about this change in your skin?
- What were you told caused it?
- Were you told not to eat certain foods?
- What did you do that helped?

If your mother said she got pimples when she was a girl, don't be upset. Almost everyone gets some, and pimples are usually temporary. If you wait a few days, they often will clear up on their own. Here are some things you can do to help keep the pores from clogging in the first place:

- Try washing your face two or three times a day with a mild soap designed for oily skin. Be sure not to scrub your skin.

- Choose a hairstyle that keeps your hair away from your face if you can. Hair simply adds more oils to the surface of your skin.

- Never squeeze a pimple or pick it open. It can cause your skin to get infected or make painful cysts develop below the surface of the skin. And it can leave scars that will be there your whole life.

- Try some of the medication you can buy in the store to help control your acne. These products work well on some pimples and can help keep pores from clogging. However, if you have red pimples that last a long time, see a physician for treatment. Doctors who specialize in skin problems are called dermatologists. They may have medications that will help you get your acne under control.

- If you decide to start wearing makeup, read the label to be sure it does not have oil in it. The oils in some makeup can clog your pores even more. The same is true of skin creams.

Nobody likes to get pimples, but it helps to know that they are temporary and that *you* will notice your pimples a lot more than anyone else will. It is also true that boys usually get more acne than girls, and girls who have oily skin tend to get fewer wrinkles later in life.

The sun can affect your skin, too. Some people like the way their skin looks after a summer in the sun. A little bit of sun can help dry up the oils in your skin that cause acne. But the sun's rays—the ultraviolet ones—can be very dangerous. They can cause sunburns that get red and sore and then peel so that healthy skin can grow underneath. If you are light-haired or light-skinned, you will probably sunburn easier than if you have dark hair or skin. But anyone can get sunburned. A sunburn now and then may not seem like a problem. But if you are out in the sun too much, especially if you let it burn your skin a lot, you are more likely to develop skin cancer at some time in your life

To keep your skin from having problems later, avoid tanning it too much or burning it. The best thing to do is to stay in the shade as much as you can when you are outdoors. Since you can't always do that, be cautious. Use suntan lotion that has sunscreen in it to block the sun's ultraviolet rays. Be sure to put it on the bridge of your nose, the top of your ears, and under your eyes. Wear sunscreen all the time if you can, especially between eleven and three, when the sun's rays are usually the strongest. Be careful if you go to the mountains. The higher the altitude, the stronger the sun's rays will be. And don't be fooled by a cloudy day. You can get a sunburn when the sky is overcast, even in the winter. The sun's rays reflect off water, sand, and snow.

Dealing with Body Hair and Body Odor

A YEAR OR TWO after you first notice pubic hair, you will begin to grow hair under your arms. At the same time, you may notice the hair on your arms and legs get a little darker and thicker.

Some women and girls like the look of hair in their armpits and on their legs. Others do not. If the hair is bothersome to you, there are several things you can do to remove it or make it less noticeable. But you will want to discuss this with your mother. You may decide not to do anything right now.

Most women who want to remove hair from armpits or legs prefer to simply shave it off. Some people will tell you that shaving causes the hair to grow back thicker and darker, but it doesn't. It may appear that way because as it grows back you see the thicker end of the hair shaft that was sliced off. But there isn't more hair and it isn't darker from shaving. Shaving is probably the cheapest way to remove hair. Electric shavers are more costly, but do not need their blades replaced as often as razors do. Both work well, and the choice is up to you.

Another way people remove hair is to use a special wax. It is spread over the area and then pulled off when it hardens, taking the hair with it. As you might have guessed, this method can be pretty uncomfortable! There are also depilatory creams that can be spread over the hair and left for a few

---

DAUGHTERS:

- Ask your mother if she removes hair from her armpits or legs.
- How does she do it?
- When did she start removing hair?
- What would she suggest you use if you want to remove hair?
- What age does she think would be a good time for you to start removing hair?

---

minutes to eat away at the hair roots. Then the hair just wipes away. Both waxing and depilatory creams work, but they can irritate your skin. It is a good idea to try them on only a small area first. And remember, neither of these methods removes the hair forever. The only permanent hair removal process is called electrolysis. It involves burning the roots of each hair, one by one, with a needle. It is an uncomfortable and expensive option.

About the same time you develop hair in your armpits, you will probably notice wetness or sweat in this area—especially when you are nervous or when you exercise. You may notice the same thing on the palms of your hands, the bottom of your feet, and between your legs. This is because the sweat glands in your body mature during puberty. Sweat usually does not smell bad unless it comes in contact with bacteria on the skin. Washing with soap is the best way to remove bacteria. And since bacteria forms all over your body after just a few hours, you may need to take a bath or shower each day to keep your skin clean and to avoid smelling.

If you notice that regular bathing is not enough to stop your underarm odor, you will want to use a deodorant to cover the odor and an antiperspirant to stop the wetness. Many underarm products have both a deodorant and an antiperspirant in them, but you will want to know what you are buying. Be sure not to use any of these products between your legs. They may irritate your skin. Just wash that area daily with mild soap. You can also reduce wetness and odor by wearing shirts, blouses, and underwear made from natural fibers like cotton. If you notice a strong odor or itching in your vaginal area, you could have an overgrowth of bacteria in this area or an infection. Infections sometimes need medicine to get them under control. Be sure to tell your mother so she can talk to your doctor.

Deciding What to Eat

WHAT YOU EAT is important, and not just because some things taste better than others! After all, the food you eat supplies your body with the nutrients it needs for energy and to grow and develop normally. Eating the right foods can even help you prevent and fight off illness.

Your body naturally knows how much food it needs to stay close to its normal weight, but you have to be careful to eat the food that will give you the right nutrients. People who care about you may tell you not to eat too many snack foods or drink too many soft drinks. They may say it so often that you get tired of hearing it. But there is a good reason for their concern. Snack foods often do not have the protein, fiber, vitamins, and minerals you need to stay healthy. Snack food, like more nutritious food, can end your hunger. But if you eat junk food instead of food with nutrients, your body will get less and less healthy over time.

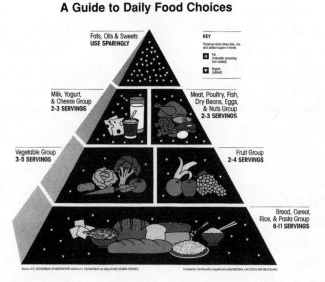

Food Guide Pyramid
A Guide to Daily Food Choices

Figure 4

MOTHERS AND DAUGHTERS:

- List all the foods you ate today.

- Did you eat several servings from each food group?

- Is there anything you think you should eat more or less of?

Your mother has probably talked about eating balanced meals. She is saying that she wants to get the right nutrients through the food she eats. It is not as difficult as it may sound. Look at the Food Pyramid in Figure 4. This chart groups together the foods that give you certain kinds of nutrients. It tells how many servings of each group you should eat each day in order to get what your body needs. Your body needs a lot of the foods at the bottom of the pyramid. Foods near the top have fewer nutrients, and your body doesn't need as much of them. But you need foods from every part of the pyramid to stay healthy.

You may notice as you go through puberty that you are hungrier than you used to be. That is only natural. A growing body needs more energy. As your body becomes more like that of an adult woman, your breasts will develop and your hips widen. This frightens some girls into thinking they are getting fat. Don't worry. These changes are perfectly normal. You will need to reach the weight that is right for your body in order to start your periods, and that means you may need to eat more during this time. Trying to stop the way your body is developing by dieting or not eating can be harmful to your health.

Unless you are seriously overweight, dieting is not for you. Crash diets and fad diets are particularly dangerous. Many of them suggest that you should eat all of one thing or none of another. This can cause you not to get the right nutrients. The diets that promise to work quickly don't work in the long run. Usually they make you lose the liquid that is in the cells in your body, so the weight you lose in the first week or so is water weight. It will come right back when you eat normally again. And cutting way back on the amount of food you eat is a sure way to miss out on the nutrients you need.

If you are truly overweight, the most sensible thing to do is to make sure you are eating the variety of foods suggested by the food pyramid. Eat three meals a day and make a goal of gradual weight loss. Skipping meals, especially breakfast, could actually make you eat more when you are overly hungry later. Skipping meals and making drastic cuts in the amount you eat can also make your body use food more slowly. Instead, try getting more exercise and eating less junk food. Pay no attention to advice from people selling a specific diet product or program, and ask a physician to help you set healthy goals for your weight loss.

MOTHERS AND DAUGHTERS:

• Talk about any silly diets you have heard of.

• What do they tell you to eat or not eat?

• What do they say will happen?

• What makes them a bad idea?

Getting Your Exercise

PEOPLE WHO ARE physically active are generally healthier than people who are not active. Exercise makes them strong, it reduces their stress, and they get sick less often than people who are not active. They even tend to live longer. Your muscles need to be used in order to stay strong and healthy. And your heart is a muscle just like the muscles in your arms and legs—except it works without your having to think about it. Your arms and legs get stronger when you use them, and the same is true of your heart. Activities that make you breathe hard, or aerobic exercise, make the heart more efficient and better conditioned. Of course, you should talk to your doctor before you make any big changes in your level or type of exercise.

MOTHERS AND DAUGHTERS:

- Name some activities you do that exercise your arms and legs.
- Name some activities that require you to breathe hard.

Many teenagers get enough exercise through sports and recreational activities like bicycling, running, or team sports. But some are less active than they were when they were younger; they spend more time watching television or talking on the phone than exercising. It is possible to do some of both. And many people are surprised that they feel more energetic when they are active.

If you find that you are sitting more than you are walking

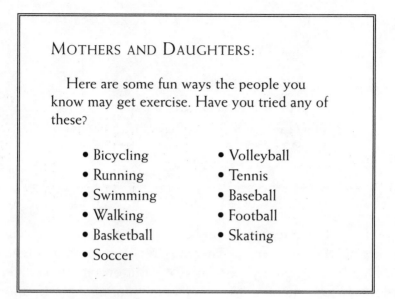

MOTHERS AND DAUGHTERS:

Here are some fun ways the people you know may get exercise. Have you tried any of these?

- Bicycling
- Running
- Swimming
- Walking
- Basketball
- Soccer

- Volleyball
- Tennis
- Baseball
- Football
- Skating

or that you are inside your house more than outside, you might want to increase your level of activity. There are many ways to get exercise without it seeming like work. The trick is to find things you like to do and let the exercise entertain you.

Remember, more is not always better. Generally, exercise that works your heart for thirty minutes three times a week is good for you. Some people do much more than that when they train for sports. But frequent, intense exercise should be done under the supervision of a coach or certified athletic trainer. Exercising too heavily or too frequently can overtire you, cause injuries, make you lose sleep, and even make you feel depressed.

Getting a Good Night's Sleep

SOME PEOPLE NEED more sleep than others. But everyone needs to get enough of it in order to feel alert and energetic during

---

MOTHERS AND DAUGHTERS:

• How much sleep do you get most nights?
• Do you think it is enough? Why or why not?
• How can you tell if you haven't had enough
  sleep?

---

the day. As a preteen, you probably need about nine or ten
hours of sleep each night. This may decrease to about eight
or nine hours during your teen years. But everybody is different. Pay close attention to how you feel during the day, and
adjust your bedtime accordingly. Sleep-overs and slumber
parties are fun, and a late night now and then won't hurt
you. But cutting your sleep short too often can make you
tired and crabby, and cause you to have trouble concentrat-
ing. And remember that caffeine (which is in chocolate and
many soft drinks), some medications, and stress can keep
you up at night.

Handling Stress

MANY GIRLS THINK all the talk about being stressed out
doesn't apply to them. Stress is being worried, nervous,
or excited about something. And you can tell when you
are feeling stressed if you pay attention to your body.
Sometimes you get butterflies in your stomach. You may
feel your muscles get tense, or the palms of your hands get
sweaty. You may notice that your heart beats faster or your
breathing speeds up. And sometimes you may even have

MOTHERS AND DAUGHTERS:

Take turns telling each other about a time when you felt stressed. (Mothers, think of times when you were your daughter's age.) Think of happy times and difficult times. How did you know you were stressed? Did you notice any of the following changes in your body?

- Sweaty palms
- Difficulty breathing
- Butterflies in your stomach
- Rapid heartbeat
- Loss of appetite
- Problems sleeping
- Tight muscles
- Headache
- Sweaty armpits

trouble eating or sleeping. All these are your body's ways of indicating stress.

We usually think of stress as being caused by things we don't like, such as taking a test, arguing with friends, or getting a shot at the doctor's office. But stress can also occur when good things happen. Going to a party, making new friends, or moving to a new city can cause stress, even though all of those things may be wonderful. A little bit of stress can be fine; it can even make you do better on a test. But stress adds up. Too much stress over too long a time can make you tired and cranky. And it can make your body sick—with a stomachache or a headache or even a cold.

The signs of stress are normal. They are your body's way of getting ready for the challenges that are causing the stress. And everyone has stress in their lives. But when you get nervous or anxious a lot or stay that way for a long time, it is time to think about taking better care of yourself. Paying attention to the signs your body gives you can tell you when you need to slow down or relax a little. Here are some things you can do to keep stress from hurting your health. They can help you relax, and give your mind and body a chance to recover from stress.

1. *Close your eyes and imagine a place you have been that was relaxing.* (Some people picture a beach on a sunny day, or a walk in the woods, or a cozy chair at Grandma's house.) Imagine every detail you can in your picture. Include the colors and sounds of the place. Try to remember what it feels like to be there.

2. *Practice breathing deeply.* When we are stressed we tend to hold our breath or breathe shallowly. Take several slow, deep breaths in a row to help your body relax. Count to five as you breathe in through your nose, hold your breath briefly, then breathe out through your mouth as you count to five again.

3. *Learn to relax your muscles.* When we are stressed we tighten our muscles without even realizing it. Then we get sore muscles, headaches, or stiff necks, and sleeping can be difficult. Try sitting or lying down in a comfortable position and closing your eyes. Tighten the muscles in one part of your body and keep them tight for a minute. Feel what they are like when they are tense. Then let them go as limp as possible. Do this with your legs, buttocks, stomach, shoulders, arms, hands, neck, and head. Then sit or lie still for a few minutes with everything just as relaxed as you can get it. If

someone were to pick up your arm at this point and let go, it should fall loosely to your side.

4. *Get plenty of sleep.* If you find it hard to go to sleep, try thinking of something you did during the day that was pleasant or perhaps boring. Picture yourself going through the motions again very slowly. Or think of something that you might repeat over and over such as counting sheep or counting backward from 200. I sometimes suggest thinking of a compound word or pair of words like *raindrop* and then trying to think of another word that starts with the end of the one before it—for example, *raindrop . . . dropkick . . . kick-off,* and so forth, just to see how far I can go. If you get stuck, start over with a new word or pick one that rhymes instead. This jumbles your thoughts and keeps you from thinking about things that might be worrying you.

5. *Get some exercise.* A brisk walk outdoors or a fast game of soccer can do wonders for those tight muscles or worries. Getting outside can be refreshing. Try to do some form of exercise that works your heart several times each week.

6. *Talk about what is bothering you.* Saying it out loud can help you find answers to problems or simply make you feel better. When you are feeling stressed, try talking to your mother.

Feeling Good

THE CHANGES YOUR body goes through during puberty can seem pretty unusual. Your body hasn't changed this much this fast since you were a baby! It can seem like a lot to think about, but you will get used to it. Taking care of yourself will become natural after a while. Just be careful not to take these changes too seriously. Everyone's body matures. These things are not a secret. You don't need to be embarrassed to buy deodorant or feminine napkins or tampons at the drugstore or supermarket.

If possible, try not to get too preoccupied with how you look. You want to look nice, of course, and stay clean. But don't let yourself think that everybody is looking at you or judging your appearance. That simply isn't true. Thinking that way can make it hard to relax and be yourself. Be proud of your body and enjoy your ability to do things with it. Dance, play an instrument, or join a team sport. None of these changes should get in your way at all. You are growing and getting stronger every day, and that is something to celebrate.

CHAPTER 5

You Sure Are Moody!

You will feel good most of the time while you are growing up. Your body is young and strong, and you have a lot to look forward to. But during puberty you may also find that your energy and moods change suddenly. You may go from happy to sad—or from silly to embarrassed—and back again in a very short time.

The changes that are going on in your body can have a lot to do with these ups and downs. Remember that your brain is sending out hormones to tell your body to grow and develop. These hormones change during the month to tell your ovaries to release an egg and to get your uterus ready to receive it. Hormones can affect how you feel physically—for example, whether you are tired or your breasts are sore. And they can affect how you feel emotionally—whether you are happy or sad or angry or scared. Because of hormones, many women find that they are more sensitive or grouchy the week before or during their period. They get angry or cry more easily than usual. Of course, not every woman experiences these changes. And not every bad mood is caused by hormones.

DAUGHTERS:

Ask your mother:

- Do you think your moods are affected by your periods?
- How do your moods change?
- When do you notice your moods most?
- What makes you feel better when you feel moody?

Managing Your Moods

EVERYONE FEELS MOODY at times, mothers and daughters alike. You may surprise yourself by snapping at someone you aren't really mad at or by crying at things that wouldn't ordinarily make you cry. You may feel like you are on a roller-coaster with your moods. Whether your moods are caused by changes in hormones or not, here are some things you can do that may help you feel better and keep you from hurting other peoples' feelings or making the situation worse.

1. *Figure out what kind of mood you are in.* This is not always as easy as it sounds. You can have several feelings at once. For example, let's say that you forgot to take a homework assignment to school. You might be scared that you will get into trouble, angry at yourself for forgetting it, irritated with your friends for asking about it, and embarrassed that others know you forgot it. That's a lot of feelings to have all at once!

MOTHERS AND DAUGHTERS:

For each face below, pick all the feelings from the list that could possibly go with it.

Happy   Frustrated
Sad   Afraid
Angry   Guilty
Disappointed   Jealous
Tired   Embarrassed
Bored   Nervous

You probably noticed that several of the feelings in the feelings exercise could go with more than one face. And some of the feelings you listed for any given face may not even go together. You can't always tell how someone is feeling just by looking.

2. *Tell the people around you how you are feeling.* This is very difficult for some people. When you are experiencing a strong emotion, you might think that others should just *know*

MOTHERS AND DAUGHTERS:

Practice telling each other how you feel. Take turns putting a feeling in this sentence and finishing it with a situation in which you have had that feeling. Try choosing other feelings from the list below.

I feel _____ when this happens: _____

Happy	Frustrated
Sad	Worried
Angry	Satisfied
Excited	Successful
Disappointed	Afraid
Scared	Guilty
Tired	Embarrassed
Bored	

---

how you feel, that you shouldn't have to tell them. But they can be wrong about how you are feeling if you leave it up to them to figure it out. Just as you couldn't be sure which feelings should go with the pictures, others can guess your feelings only from how you look and what you do. You could have a frown on your face because you are very sad about something, and someone looking at you could think you were mad at her. She could go away with her feelings hurt or angry at you rather than trying to help you feel better.

When you are feeling bad, you may not feel like telling other people exactly what is wrong at that moment. You may need time to think about the situation, or it may be too personal to share with them. You should still let them know how you are feeling so they don't get the wrong idea. Tell them you don't want to talk about what is wrong by saying something like "I'm in a really bad mood, but it's nothing you did. I don't want to get mad at you, so could you leave me alone for a little while?"

3. *Tell others what you need from them.* Even if you tell other people how you are feeling, don't expect them to automatically know what to do about it. They may try their best to help and do absolutely the wrong thing. For instance, if you say, "I'm sad right now," they could think the best thing to do is to leave you alone. But you might need and want their company! You might have to let them know what you want them to do. If you want to be left alone, be sure to tell them in a polite way. When we are upset it is easy to yell at other people. If you say, "I'm feeling angry right now and would like to be alone for a little while," this gives them a greater understanding of the situation. Getting into an argument would only make the situation worse.

4. *Rethink the situation.* Sometimes it isn't a good idea to trust your reactions to things when you are in a bad mood. If

you are feeling sad or angry or frustrated, you will look at the world differently than when you are having a better day. When you feel happy, someone who normally bugs you may be easier to take. When you feel angry or sad, even your best friend's funny comments may seem boring or insulting. It is easy to jump to conclusions or make a big problem out of a little one if you don't rethink the situation.

Rethinking is just what it sounds like: thinking again. When we are upset, we often make a snap judgment about what's going on and how to handle it. And our first thoughts may not be right. For instance, you could think, "I forgot to bring my homework to school. That is bad because my teacher will think I am stupid. I feel like not trying anymore. I'm going to quit school." See how easy it is to talk yourself into giving up? Learning to rethink situations can keep you from making the wrong decision. It opens your mind to other possibilities: Maybe what happened isn't so bad. And maybe it can be fixed.

Rethinking Your Problems

I ONCE MET a girl named Karen who made a big problem out of a little one because she didn't stop to rethink her situation. Karen had been best friends with Sara for eight years. They did everything together and everyone called them "the twins," even though they weren't even sisters. One day a new girl, Kim, started at their school, and they both liked her. The next Monday, someone told Karen that she had seen Sara and Kim at the mall together on Saturday. Because Karen hadn't been invited, she immediately thought that Sara liked the new girl better than her. She was afraid she would lose her best friend. So when Sara called that night, Karen was snippy with her and hung up on her. And she hung up the next three times Sara called her. Here's how Karen's thinking went:

What happened:	Sara went shopping with Kim.
Karen's first thought:	"Sara doesn't like me anymore."
She felt:	Angry and hurt
She acted:	Angry—she hung up on her friend.

Well, you can guess what happened next. Sara quit calling or even talking to Karen. She felt hurt and angry herself and started spending more time with Kim because Karen was being rude. Karen was making her first thought—that Sara liked Kim better than her—come true by believing it and acting like it was true.

Karen and I talked about rethinking. She learned that rethinking means not trusting your first reaction to a situation. It means making yourself wonder if there are different conclusions you can draw from whatever is happening. Karen thought back to when she found out Sara and Kim had gone shopping. She listed some of the things she *could* have thought instead of deciding that Sara didn't like her anymore. She tried to think of other things that could have explained the situation. Here's the list she came up with:

Maybe Kim invited Sara to shop.
Maybe they tried to call me and I wasn't home.
Maybe Sara's mother wanted her to just have one
    friend along.
Maybe it didn't mean anything.

You can probably think of other possibilities. When Karen thought it over, she realized that rethinking the situation was a good idea. She found that it pays to rethink if we

MOTHERS AND DAUGHTERS:

Tell each other about a time when you jumped to a conclusion you later found out was not correct.

• What happened?
• What conclusion did you come to?
• What else might you have thought of if you had done some rethinking?
• How would it have turned out differently?

don't want to make our first—and usually worst—thoughts come true! Karen apologized to Sara and things got better. But guess what Sara and Kim were doing at the store that weekend: They were buying a birthday present for Karen! That was a possibility she hadn't even thought of.

Here is another example of a situation where rethinking would have helped things turn out differently. It involved a girl named Brenda. Like many girls who are going through puberty, Brenda worried about how she looked. She felt self-conscious because her body was changing, and she thought everyone was looking at her and picking out her flaws. She didn't realize that that simply isn't true. She learned the hard way that nobody pays as much attention to how you look as you do. Friends like you for who you are, not what you look like.

Brenda had a pimple on her chin one day. She felt sad and embarrassed and didn't want to be around her friends. She told herself she was ugly. She decided that the pimple was the only thing people would notice about her, and that they would make fun of her for it. She went to school that day and thought everybody was staring at her. She acted shy and wouldn't talk to anyone. Her friends couldn't figure out why she was being so rude. They didn't enjoy being with her like they usually did, and they avoided her because of her behavior. They didn't notice her pimple, but she was sure that was why they stayed away. She acted uncomfortable and rude, and her behavior made others feel uncomfortable and angry.

See how it goes? If you think something bad about yourself, you feel angry or hurt or embarrassed. When you act different in some way that others don't enjoy, they avoid you or get angry. Then you decide you were right about what you were thinking about yourself! This can be a vicious cycle. Sometimes we just have to fight the way our feelings make us want to act, and act like we are happier than we are. That can be all it takes to convince yourself or others that things are going to be okay. And it keeps them from reacting to you in a way you'll be sorry for later.

What if Brenda had done things differently? She could have told herself that her thoughts—about her friends hating her because of her pimple—weren't true. She could have decided to behave as though the pimple weren't even there. Then nobody would have gotten annoyed with her. And she would have found out that her pimple didn't matter to them at all.

Here's the way it went the first time around:

She thought:	"They won't like me, I'm ugly."
She felt:	Self-conscious and angry
She behaved:	Angry, not sociable
Others reacted:	Annoyed, angry, withdrawn
She thought:	"I was right, I'm ugly. No one likes me."

Here's the difference rethinking would have made:

She would think:	"They won't like me, I'm ugly."
She would *rethink:*	"This pimple probably won't make any difference to them."
She would feel:	Self-conscious but more confident
She would act:	Sociable and normal
Others would react:	Sociable and normal
She would think:	"I was right, it didn't matter to them at all."

MOTHERS AND DAUGHTERS:

Think of a time recently when you had strong feelings about something that happened and then did some rethinking that changed the way you responded. Fill in the blanks below as if you were in the situation again.

I felt_____ because_____ happened.
At first I thought it was terrible because _____
_____.

I wanted to _____.

But I did a rethink.

I thought, "It is also possible that _____."
So I _____.

The key to not overreacting in any situation is to rethink and act confident. It can make a big difference in how things turn out!

What to Do When You Are Feeling Bad

IN ADDITION TO rethinking, there are other things you can do to help yourself feel better when you are sad or angry. When you are upset, try several of these approaches to see which ones work best for you.

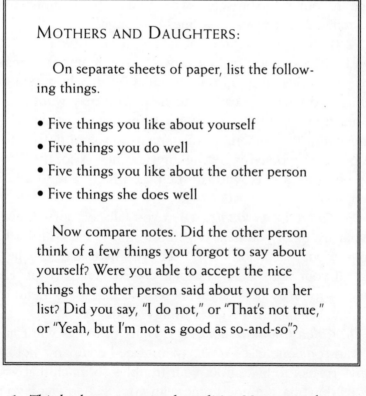

MOTHERS AND DAUGHTERS:

On separate sheets of paper, list the following things.

- Five things you like about yourself
- Five things you do well
- Five things you like about the other person
- Five things she does well

Now compare notes. Did the other person think of a few things you forgot to say about yourself? Were you able to accept the nice things the other person said about you on her list? Did you say, "I do not," or "That's not true," or "Yeah, but I'm not as good as so-and-so"?

1. *Think about your good qualities.* Many people never stop to think about the things they like about themselves or

why other people like them. Then when things don't go well at home or school, they can't come up with a single good thought about themselves. They blow things out of proportion and decide they are no good altogether. They act like their own worst enemy!

A lot of people have trouble accepting compliments. It embarrasses them and they don't know what to do, so they say things that make the compliment seem untrue. Then the giver feels uncomfortable, too. It is okay to feel good about yourself. Try simply saying, "Thank you." Or give the other person a compliment if you can think of one: "You're pretty good at that yourself." But don't feel like you should convince the other person she is wrong! Keep the compliment. And remember it whenever times get tough.

2. *Talk to your mother.* Your mother can be a great friend when you are feeling down. Just remember to make sure you choose a good time to talk. Tell her how you are feeling and what she can do to help. You may want to ask for her opinion. Or you may just want her to listen and understand. But remember to remain calm and not make the problem worse by getting angry at her. Also, there may be other adults who can help you feel better. Call on them, too.

3. *Call a friend to talk.* When you talk to yourself, even in your head, all you hear is yourself. If you tell yourself bad things about a situation or yourself, you may start to believe them. If your self-speech is negative—like "I'm bad" or "I'm dumb"—you may need someone else to talk to. A friend can help you remember the good things about you.

4. *Call a friend for company.* Think of things you can do with someone else. You may just need company, not sympathy. Try not to talk about your troubles so much that your friends don't have a good time with you. Rather, enjoy your time with them.

5. *Do something else for a while.* If you stay by yourself when you are upset, you can talk yourself into feeling worse. You may need to do something else to forget your troubles for a while. Set your concerns aside to think about at a later time, and find something else to occupy your thoughts.

6. *Get some exercise.* Remember, the outdoors can make you feel good and relieve stress. Bicycle, walk, run, or play a sport. Celebrate how your body moves. And be sure to take in the scenery!

7. *Write your feelings down.* Keeping a journal can be a helpful way to sort out your feelings. Find a notebook or a tablet, and use it to write your thoughts or feelings whenever your feelings get strong. When you put your feelings down on paper, you get rid of them for a while. You can say things in your journal you aren't sure you should say to another person, and writing might help you decide what to do.

8. *Pamper yourself.* When it feels like no one else cares (which is never quite true) it is time to be nice to yourself, not nasty. Do something just to be nice to *you.* Watch a favorite movie. Read a good book. Take a hot bath. Relax.

9. *Laugh a little.* Things are seldom as serious as they seem, and laughing a little can help relieve the tension. Try rewatching your favorite comedy. Call someone who is fun to be with. You might even be able to find something funny about your situation and make a joke about it.

10. *Help someone less fortunate than you are.* Sometimes we can feel too sorry for ourselves; we forget that things could be much worse. When you are feeling sad, remember that there are others who could probably use *your* help. Try doing something nice for them. Giving your time or attention to someone else can make you feel better, too. A good deed can be as involved as visiting someone in a nursing home or as simple as helping a neighbor carry groceries. Opportunities are everywhere.

11. *Be a kid a while longer (or act like one if you are a mother)*. Sometimes we try to grow up too fast or to act grown up all the time. But it can be healthy to relax and be just plain silly once in a while. Even when you are a teenager or a grown-up, it is okay to act like a kid now and then and do kid things. Play with your dolls, dig out your old toys, laugh with your little sister, or hug your stuffed animal. It can help when you are feeling blue.

12. *Ask for a hug*. Others don't always know when you need one of these. Don't be afraid to say, "I could use a hug." Could you use one now?

13. *Think about the good things ahead*. There are always things to look forward to; you could probably make a long list if you tried. These may be big things such as summer vacation or a part in the school play. Or they may be small ones, such as having your favorite meal or getting to sleep in on Saturday morning. No matter how big or small your future plans are, keeping them in mind can help get you past the difficult times.

MOTHERS AND DAUGHTERS:

Take turns finishing these sentences:

Tomorrow I am looking forward to _____
_____.

Next week I am looking forward to _____
_____.

Someday I am looking forward to _____
_____.

---

14. *Ask for help.* If you are in a sad or angry mood a lot of the time, it is bound to interfere with your life. It can be hard to make or keep friends, or to have a good time with your family. A psychologist or other trained professional can help you think through problems or discuss them with others involved. Don't be afraid to suggest the idea to your parent.

CHAPTER 6

What You See and Hear Outside Your Home

How DO WE know what to do in different situations? How do we know how to act around other people? It is not something we learn in a day. We learn gradually from the people around us. We watch the people who care about us—parents, relatives, and teachers—and learn from what they say and do. But there are many other people who would like to tell us how to act—people who don't necessarily care about us. In fact, they don't even know us. They are the people we see and hear in the media—on the television, on the radio, and in written materials. They give us powerful messages about how to look, feel, and act. And their advice is not always the best advice.

For the most part, news reporters try to be unbiased, accurate, and even helpful. But a lot of media messages don't even try to be helpful. Some messages give you the wrong advice—advice that doesn't help you in any way or could actually harm you, such as telling you to buy cigarettes or alcohol. Why do people do that? The reason is simple: They are trying to make money.

MOTHERS AND DAUGHTERS:

Pick two or three of the types of media below. Can you remember anything they tried to get you to do?

- A television show or commercial
- A newspaper article or advertisement
- A radio show or announcer
- A billboard
- A song
- A book
- The Internet
- A magazine article or advertisement
- An entertainer (singer, comedian, etc.)

One way media people make money is by entertaining you. If an article or song or story looks like it will be fun or interesting, you are more likely to buy the magazine or album or book it is in. Another way they make money is by selling the products they advertise, such as cigarettes or soap or toys. Every time you buy a product that has been on a commercial or in an advertisement, part of the money you spend goes to pay the people who helped convince you to buy it.

A lot of magazines, movies, and billboards show you unhealthy ways to act or try to get you to buy something. And you can't avoid seeing them. But the good news is,

No matter what you see or hear in the media, you don't have to agree with it! And you don't have to do what it suggests! You can make your own decisions.

Sometimes you can even learn what *not* to do from the media. Your job is to filter through all their messages and decide for yourself what to do or how to act. That means you have to watch, read, and listen with a little bit of doubt. You have to question the messages the media are sending. As my father used to say, "Don't believe everything you hear and only half of what you see." Sometimes it is hard to know what to believe or what is right for you, especially when the media are working so hard and spending so much money to do your thinking for you. That's a time when a mother-daughter talk can help sort things out.

What Have You Seen So Far?

MOTHERS, YOU HAVE had a lot of practice deciding what to believe and how to behave. By the time you became an adult

---

MOTHERS:

Think back to when you were a girl:

• Can you name something you saw someone do on television that wasn't a good idea for you to do?

• Can you name something you bought that didn't turn out the way the advertisement suggested it would?

---

you probably heard hundreds of television or radio shows and read thousands of advertisements. But everyone learns a few things the hard way. And somewhere along the way you probably listened to some not so good advice from the media.

Being a grown woman doesn't stop the media from sending you messages. You just learn to ignore a lot of them. But you are so used to ignoring them that you might forget your daughter may be hearing them for the first time and taking them seriously. The only way to know what messages she is getting is sometimes to watch the shows she watches, listen to her music, and read some of her magazines. She would probably like to share them with you if you are interested. The media can give you a lot to talk about together.

MOTHERS AND DAUGHTERS:

Take turns telling each other about these media:

- Name a television show you have seen. Tell something that happened in one of the episodes.
- Name a song your friends like. Does it give you any ideas about how to behave?
- Name a fairy tale you heard when you were younger. How did the girl act?
- Name your favorite commercial. What is it selling? How does it make you want to buy it?
- Name a magazine that your friends read. Why do you think they like it?

The Messages Your Entertainment Sends

LIKE MOST PEOPLE, you probably use the media for entertainment. You watch television or go to the movies or read books. You may like funny stories or serious ones, scary stories or mysteries. Whatever you choose to watch or read, there is a good chance that the main character in it is a girl or woman the same age as or a little older than you are. That is because we like to imagine what it would be like to be someone else—someone who is different but similar enough to us that it could be possible. We put ourselves in her place, think about the problems she faces, and watch how she goes about solving them. We learn about that character's way of thinking, and if we like her, we may want to act like her. If we aren't careful, we can believe that her way of behaving is great, without thinking about whether it is the right way for us.

MOTHERS AND DAUGHTERS:

Think of a show, movie, or book you both have seen that had a girl or woman as the main character.

- Did you like her?
- Did you feel happy or sad or angry for her?
- Do you think you would like to be like her?
- How?
- How would you want to be different?

The media can sometimes give you good ideas about
how to act with other people. But many of the things you see
and hear probably don't fit with the way things are in your
life. You have your own ideas about how to behave. Your
family has rules about how people are supposed to treat each
other and ways of showing that you care about each other,
and you are not supposed to do certain things. Characters on
television or in books don't necessarily act like your family
members. If people in the media seem to have a better life or
more fun, you may think there is something wrong with your
life. And that is true for both mothers and daughters. You may
feel that you should act like the people in the show, but be
careful—remember they are making money by entertaining
you. You may be getting ideas that are not so good about
how to treat other people, how to treat yourself, and how to
let other people treat you.

MOTHERS AND DAUGHTERS:

Take turns thinking of a situation in a movie
you watched or a book you read where people
did things that are not okay at your house.
How would you have handled it differently?

Messages About How to Treat Other People. Some
people on television and in the movies are nice to each other,
and some aren't. Some joke around in harmless ways; others
do or say rude things. They make fun of other people, talk
back to parents, or play mean tricks on each other. Such actions
may be funny to watch, but it isn't funny to actually treat other

people that way. And you wouldn't think it was so funny if they did it to you. It is one thing to laugh at things when they are make-believe, and another thing to do them yourself. It is important to keep the difference firmly in your mind.

MOTHERS AND DAUGHTERS:

Take turns thinking of a situation in a movie or TV show that you laughed at, but that you would not want to be part of. Why would you not want to treat people that way?

Messages About How to Treat Yourself. Not only do people in the media sometimes treat other people badly, they are not always nice to themselves. They do things that are dangerous, such as drinking or smoking or taking drugs. They take risks that look fun and exciting on the screen, but could kill a person if done in real life. You wouldn't try most of them. But when I was very little I thought maybe I could fly like the cartoon character Mighty Mouse—or at least I thought it was worth trying. I jumped off my dresser, and I didn't fly very far! But I did learn a valuable lesson about not believing everything I see.

Characters in the movies and on TV sometimes drive faster than they should, leave their seat belts unfastened, or even play with guns. Sometimes these behaviors are shown as normal or even good. The media can make characters seem smart or strong or exciting when they don't take care of themselves. But remember, the characters don't have to worry about getting hurt because they are played by actors. Everything they do is make-believe. The real world doesn't work the same way.

MOTHERS AND DAUGHTERS:

Take turns thinking of a situation in a movie or TV show where the characters did things that were dangerous or not healthy. Why would you not do them?

Messages About How to Let Others Treat You. The characters in shows or stories don't always make sure that other people treat them well, either. For some reason, girls and women especially seem to let others do things to them or for them, rather than taking care of things themselves. Think about the fairy tales you have heard. A girl or woman usually faces some kind of problem, but she isn't usually the one who solves it. In "Snow White," for example, the problem is that Snow White is so beautiful the wicked stepmother wants to kill her. She runs away, does foolish things like letting a stranger in the front door and eating a poisoned apple, and finally is rescued by a handsome man. What a message to give girls: Let yourself be treated like you are dumb or helpless, and wait for a man to fix your problem!

Females in stories and shows often try very hard to get a boyfriend or a husband. They make it seem like women are not okay unless they have a male to take care of them. And they sometimes do strange things to try to get one. The things they do may hurt themselves or someone else—

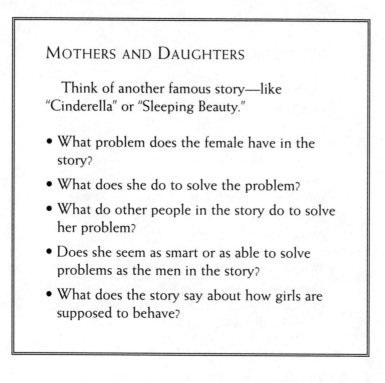

MOTHERS AND DAUGHTERS

Think of another famous story—like "Cinderella" or "Sleeping Beauty."

• What problem does the female have in the story?

• What does she do to solve the problem?

• What do other people in the story do to solve her problem?

• Does she seem as smart or as able to solve problems as the men in the story?

• What does the story say about how girls are supposed to behave?

like lying to their friends or acting different than they really are. Some of their behavior is more childish than that of young children. But some people find it funny because it is entertaining.

In real life, a lot of women don't have husbands or boyfriends and are happy. They have friends they care about, male and female, who treat them well. Fortunately, some shows are starting to show women as being able to take care of themselves. And some of them show women who solve problems as well as men. They don't need to act helpless, and their friends like that about them. As you watch or read, it is important to think about what the story tells you about how to act as a female.

MOTHERS AND DAUGHTERS:

Think again about the television show or movie that had a girl as an important character.

- How did the people treat each other? Were they nice to each other or rude? Were they honest or did they trick each other? How is it different at your house? Who in the show would you want for a friend? What would make him or her a good friend?

- What problem did the girl face in the show? How was it solved? Did she solve it herself or did someone else do it for her? Do you think what she did is a good way for a girl to behave?

- Did the actors and actresses do anything dangerous?

Advertisements Send Messages, Too

ADVERTISEMENTS APPEAR in a lot of forms: in magazines, on the radio, and in commercials on television. They are all trying to sell you something or change the way you act. Television has an advantage over the other media because it can show *and* tell its messages at the same time. But advertisements in any of the media do similar things to get you to want to buy a product.

1. *They make the product seem cool.* You are no doubt wiser about what to believe than you used to be. You know that advertisements don't always show things that are real. When you were little you might have believed that plastic models could fly around the world or that dolls could dance like real people just because it looked that way on TV. You might have thought people's eyes could pop into pinwheels or smoke could come from their ears the way the media showed it. Commercials can make products look like they do amazing things—like move really fast or blow up or disappear. But at your age, you know that some products don't do everything it looks like they do. And even though they may taste good or work just fine, they aren't always as great as they seem on TV.

MOTHERS AND DAUGHTERS:

- Name something you own or have tried that you see in commercials on television.
- What does the commercial do to make it seem even neater than it is?
- Is there anything it doesn't do at home that it seemed to do on television?

---

2. *They get you to remember the product.* Besides making products look extra exciting, there are other ways advertisers encourage you to buy the things they show. One of the best ways is to get you to remember the product they are selling. They want you to think about that product when you aren't watching the commercial or reading the billboard. They

know that people will sometimes remember the product just because the commercial is wacky and unrealistic, or because the people in the ad are stars, or just because people look like they are having a great time when they use whatever they are selling.

Another way commercials get people to remember a product is to use a catchy saying or slogan they hope you will remember later. And often the slogan is put in a jingle, a short verse or song with a catchy tune. Have you ever found yourself humming a commercial you just couldn't put out of your mind? Maybe you even sang it to a friend. Then they remembered the product, too! That was a pretty good commercial!

3. *They get you to use feelings, not brains.* Have you ever noticed that commercials don't tell you everything about a product? They make it hard for you to make a good decision about whether to buy it. They don't tell you that there are other products like it to choose from. They don't tell you that some people don't like the product. And they *certainly* don't remind you that if you buy it you won't have that money to buy something else you want or need. Of course not! Their

MOTHERS AND DAUGHTERS:

Take turns telling about a TV commercial or magazine advertisement that made you feel any of these ways:

- Happy
- Proud
- Jealous
- Worried
- Hungry
- Sad
- Angry
- Excited

job is to sell the product. And the more products they sell, the more money they make.

Advertisers know that we tend to compare ourselves with the people we see in the media. They know that we sometimes do what we see others doing if it looks like fun, even if we know we are watching actors and even if the actors are doing something that would not happen in real life. We sometimes buy a product we see actors use on TV just because it seems to make them feel or look great or have a lot of friends.

Commercials can try to trigger a lot of different feelings in order to get you to want what they are selling. They can make you feel hungry, jealous, excited, or even a little sad. You can want to buy what they advertise either because you like the way you are feeling or because you want to get rid of the feeling you are having. Commercials work on your *feelings,* not your brain. You have to do the thinking on your own.

4. *They make you feel bad about the way you look.* Another way advertisers use feelings to sell products is to make people feel uncomfortable or ashamed about themselves or the way they look. For example, everybody knows someone who weighs more than he or she should weigh to be healthy. But many women who are not overweight worry about getting fat when they don't need to. Advertisers try to convince even women of normal weight that they are overweight when they are not. They try to make them feel bad about themselves so they will buy things they think will make them look or feel thinner.

To do this, many advertisements use models who have dieted to be skinnier than they should be. They make it seem that these models are beautiful or happy or successful because they are so skinny. And, of course, advertisements make it look like they eat or drink or use the product they are selling in order to be that way. Often these advertisements sell foods that promise to promote weight loss so you can look like the model. The models seem to have a lot of friends (particularly boyfriends) and go to glamorous places.

MOTHERS AND DAUGHTERS:

Tell about an advertisement in a magazine or on television in which the model looks skinnier than she should be. What did you notice about her that tells you she is too thin?

You may think from all this advertising that the thinner you can be, the better. This simply is not true. Being skinny means not eating enough food, and that means not getting the right nutrition. A lot of advertisements don't give you the whole story. For example, they may tell you that by using nothing but their product you will lose weight, but they don't tell you that you will really be losing only water weight. They may tell you to lose weight in order to be more physically fit, but they don't tell you that if you lose weight too quickly you will lose muscle tissue as well as fat. You can wind up weaker by trying to be fit this way. Some girls you think look great probably believe they are fat. It is easy for them to be critical of themselves when advertisements show skinny people as having all the fun. Remember, most models are actually underweight. People who are closer to normal in their body weight are healthier, better able to get the right balance of nutrients in their diet, and likely to live longer.

Besides, excessive thinness isn't as attractive to other people as you might think. People have done studies in which boys and girls are asked to choose the girls they think are most attractive in pictures. The boys tend to choose pictures of girls that are heavier than the girls choose. This may not be true of every boy, but most of them don't think thinness is as important as girls tend to think it is. Remember, everyone's body is different. Don't let the media tell you that yours is not okay.

Other Ways the Media Affect Us

YOU ARE WISE, indeed, not to believe everything the media tell you. But even if you don't do the rude or dangerous things you see on television or read about in books, the media can

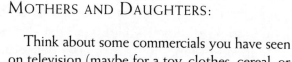

MOTHERS AND DAUGHTERS:

Think about some commercials you have seen on television (maybe for a toy, clothes, cereal, or a soft drink). Answer the following questions about them and decide for yourself which things they are doing to try to sell the product.

- Does it have a slogan or jingle?
- What does the commercial try to make you
  think will happen if you use the product?
      You will have fun.
      People will like you.
      Something cool will happen when
          you use it.
      Everybody has one.
      It does something no other one does.
      It will make you feel good.
      It will make you look great.
      It will make you rich or famous.
      You will be skinny.
      You will succeed at something.
- Do you buy this product?

affect you in other ways. Your friends listen, watch, and read the same messages you do. But they may not think about what they are hearing quite as much. They may do some of the bad things the actors or models do in the shows and advertisements. And they may try to get you to act the same way. Listen to your brain, not your feelings, and make your own decisions about how to behave.

The media can also change your family life. Some people find the media so entertaining that they watch television or read books or magazines more than they talk to other people. Any entertainment that you do all by yourself uses up time that you could spend doing the things that make your family special. Choose your entertainment wisely. Set aside a certain amount of time to read. Plan the shows you want to watch ahead of time. And remember that VCRs can let you record your favorite shows to watch later if they are on during family time.

CHAPTER 7

The Good and Not So Good Things About Friends

ONE DAY TWO GIRLS sat next to each other in my office waiting room. One had on blue jeans, wore her hair cut close to her scalp, and had three earrings in one ear. The other girl had on a pleated plaid skirt and white blouse, and wore her long dark hair in a ponytail. I remember wondering what they thought of each other because it seemed obvious to me that they were strangers (and perhaps strange) to each other. To my surprise, I later heard them talking about a party they were planning together! They told me they had been best friends for years. That experience helped me to remember that friends don't have to look alike, and that opposites can sometimes attract.

It is hard to say why we like certain people—and choose them as friends. They can think and look different from us and can come from different family situations, but something about them appeals to us. They may make us laugh. They may know things that we don't know. Or we may feel more creative when we put our ideas together with theirs. A shy person may be attracted to someone who is out-going. Someone who hates to make decisions may choose a

friend who takes the lead and comes up with ideas. Whatever it is that makes our friends fun and interesting, we enjoy
spending our free time with them.

Even though differences make friendships fun, friends
are usually alike in a lot of ways, too. They are often the
same sex and close to the same age. They usually get similar
grades in school, spend the same amount of time doing
homework, and have similar plans for going to work or college someday. And friends usually feel the same way about
important issues like cheating, stealing, or taking drugs. Even
when they disagree, real friends respect each other as people. They don't pressure each other to do things they think
are wrong or unfair. If friends don't respect each other like
this, they have a lot of disagreements and don't stay friends
very long.

What Are Friends For?

EVERYONE LOOKS FOR friends to talk to, laugh with, and share
thoughts and feelings with, and friends can be found in many
different places. You may have met your friends in your school,
church, neighborhood, or camps. Because the places we go
change from time to time, our friendships sometimes change,
too. Whenever we move or get interested in different types
of activities, we meet new people and grow apart from others.
But no matter how long friendships last, every one of them
teaches us something about ourselves.

Your friends will be especially important while you are
growing up. As you get more independent of your family you
will spend more time with your friends and be more influenced by what they say and do. At first most of your friends
will be girls; then you probably will become interested in
boys. Some boys will be just casual friends, and others you

MOTHERS AND DAUGHTERS:

Complete the following sentences about your friendships:

• My three closest friends are _____
_____.

• When I first met them, I was doing this: _____
_____.

• The friend I've had the longest is _____
_____.

• A friend that isn't nearby anymore is _____
_____.

---

may eventually go on dates with. Whether you spend your time with girls or boys, your friends will help you figure out who you are. They will help you become the person you will grow up to be.

Friends are important because they help us feel like we belong with others who are going through the same things we are. When you first start into puberty, you may feel shy about the changes you are going through. Since your friends will be going through similar changes, they will reassure you that you are okay and that the things you are experiencing are normal. They will tell you things about yourself, such as how they think you look and act, and you will do the same for them. With friends you can try out different ways of being. You can experiment with your appearance, your ideas, and your feelings, and they will help you feel good about yourself.

MOTHERS AND DAUGHTERS:

- Name something you learned about yourself from a friend.

- Did she or he tell you anything about how you look, act, or think?

As you and your friends go from having your parents' constant supervision to being on your own as young adults, you will have a lot of discussions together. Some friends talk to each other as much or more than they talk to their parents, spending time on the phone and getting together whenever they can. Be a little careful, though. I have talked to a lot of girls who feel very sad because they didn't keep time out for their family, and after a while, they didn't feel close to the family anymore. Stay connected with your family even while you get more and more independent of them.

MOTHERS:

Tell your daughter some of your feelings about her developing more friendships with girls and boys her age.

DAUGHTERS:

Tell your mother some of the reasons you need to stay close to your family as you grow up.

What Is Peer Pressure?

SOME GIRLS YOUR AGE will not be your close friends. You won't know them well or do a lot of things together, and some of them will be more popular than others. You will respect some of your popular peers; others may hurt people in order to be popular. Think about how you really want to behave before deciding that someone else's way is better. Trying too hard to be popular can sometimes have unwanted results. One girl I knew, Jenny, had nice friends she had known for years, but she talked a lot about wanting to be in the popular group in her class. These girls seemed to have a lot of fun and Jenny thought everyone wanted to be like them. The leader of the popular girls was Lori, an attractive, outspoken girl who was loud and bouncy all the time. Lori always had a small crowd around her who made fun of the girls who weren't in their group.

Even though Jenny didn't always like the way Lori behaved, she wished she got the kind of attention Lori did, and she started to think her friends were boring and uninteresting. Every day Jenny tried to get Lori's friends to accept her. She gave them a lot of attention and laughed at their jokes. She followed them around and asked to sit with them at lunch. And it worked. They finally let her sit with them, called her on the phone, and invited her to parties. But she soon found herself doing things she really didn't want to do, just so she could keep them as friends. She ignored her old friends, hated their way of dressing or acting, and made fun of them when she was around Lori. Finally, when Lori was doing poorly in school, she asked Jenny to help her cheat on a test. Jenny didn't know what to do but was afraid she would get kicked out of the group if she didn't help. She gave Lori the answers, and they both got caught. That was when Jenny finally took a hard look at the group she had joined. In trying so hard to be popular, Jenny forgot the things that were important to her—like being honest and caring about her friends. She forgot that she couldn't be close friends with everyone or even be liked by everyone. When she really thought about it, Jenny realized that she didn't have to act like anyone else to feel okay about herself. She had been a victim of negative peer pressure.

Peer pressure is the feeling that you must look a certain way or do certain things in order to be liked or accepted by others. Peers (friends or not) can influence you to do all kinds of things you wouldn't do on your own, often things that make you uncomfortable. Being made to feel uncomfortable isn't always bad. Depending on what others want you to do, their pressure might actually be good for you. If you are shy and need encouragement, your friends may push, prod, or drag you into a situation you would otherwise avoid. And you may enjoy yourself and feel more confident the next time the situation comes along.

But sometimes peer pressure isn't good. Things can get

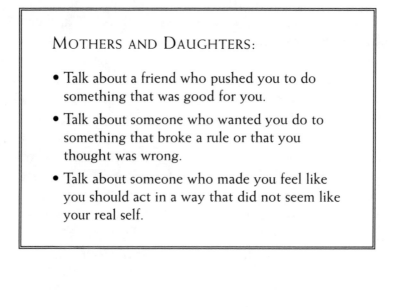

MOTHERS AND DAUGHTERS:

- Talk about a friend who pushed you to do something that was good for you.
- Talk about someone who wanted you do to something that broke a rule or that you thought was wrong.
- Talk about someone who made you feel like you should act in a way that did not seem like your real self.

a little too uncomfortable. Your peers may want you to do things that go against what you think is right or fair. Or you may feel that you have to act like them in order to get them to like you. They may make fun of you if you don't or talk you into thinking it is "grown up" to do what they say, and they may suggest things you aren't sure you really want to do. That kind of peer pressure can be difficult to deal with and can get you into trouble.

Most mothers know at least some of their daughter's peers. But they can't know everyone who influences her. They sometimes worry about that influence because they know that girls often feel pressure from other people to act a certain way. Unfortunately, girls tend to be more sensitive than boys about how they look, and they pay more attention than boys do to pleasing other people. Mothers know that people sometimes use this sensitivity to pressure girls into doing things they are told will make them more attractive or better liked—just like the advertising in the media we talked about earlier. If you are concerned about what other people

---

MOTHERS AND DAUGHTERS:

• Talk about a time when you felt like you should act or dress a certain way in order to please your friends.

• Talk about a time when someone made you think she would not like you if you didn't do something she wanted you to do. How did you feel?

think of you, they can let you believe that they would be angry or hurt if you don't go along with what they want. They can even try to make you think that you caused problems for them by not doing it. Even though mothers know that their daughters will try to make the best choices, they still worry, because peer pressure can be powerful.

Daughters sometimes feel that their mothers are too concerned about peer pressure. Daughters are growing up and want to handle situations themselves. They want their mothers to trust them to do the right thing, and they want a chance to prove their skills and judgment. Trying new responsibilities is a way to give themselves confidence and learn to handle other situations that may come up. But sometimes girls feel so defensive about wanting their mothers to know they can handle themselves that they get angry if their mothers ask about what they do with their friends. Even casual questions like "What did you do with your friends today?" seem like an interrogation. But questions like this are

---

MOTHERS AND DAUGHTERS:

- Talk about a misunderstanding you had with each other about friendships. Don't argue about it—the situation has passed.

- Take turns letting the other person say what she meant and how she felt.

- Did you learn anything new about each other by talking about it now?

not criticisms of your judgment or choice of friends. They are your mother's way of trying to learn what you think about different situations. And bringing up concerns about your friends' behaviors may be your mother's way of giving you a chance to tell her how well you can handle yourself.

Most of us are at least a little concerned about what other people think of us. We want others to like us and enjoy being around us. If we didn't care at all about their reactions we would seem self-centered or snobbish. But we can care too much about what others think. When people with the wrong ideas become too important to us, we may do what they want us to without thinking about it. Think hard about who your friends are and whether their opinions and behavior are right for you. Here are some things you can do to avoid negative peer pressure as much as possible.

- Stay involved with your family. People whose families talk to each other a lot and help each other out are better able to handle peer pressure.

- Join groups that are doing activities because you are interested in the activities the members are doing, not just because your friends are doing it.

- Look carefully at the behaviors of the people in any group you think you want to join. If you wouldn't want to act the way they do, don't work too hard to be popular with them.

- Hang around people you think do things that are right and fair. Make sure any friends who are older than you have ideas you agree with about how people should behave. Talk to your mother about the things they suggest.

If you can do these things, you will be less likely to get involved in situations where you bend to negative peer pressure. Think for yourself; do what you want to do and believe is right, not just what you think you need to do to please others.

Peer Pressure Happens to Mothers, Too

BELIEVE IT OR NOT, mothers often feel pressure to do what others want them to do. A mother has many responsibilities and other people to care for, and she often gives up things she enjoys because she is doing things for other people. This is okay if she wants to do whatever it is she is doing. But if people convince her to do things she doesn't think are right or that are harmful to her or the people she cares for, she has given in to negative peer pressure.

Mothers, you will often have to stick up for yourself or your daughter on things that have to do with her, and that isn't always easy. Back when people lived in small towns and didn't move around as much, parents knew most of what was going on in the community and among the teenagers. Towns are bigger now, and schools have more students. Your daughter's friends may come from miles away instead of living next door. You may not always meet their parents, let alone get to know them well. And when your daughter's plans or activities involve other kids, you may feel pressure not to make the special effort to talk with their parents about it. You may feel pressure to let your daughter watch movies or go to parties you're not comfortable with because other parents are letting their kids do it. But they may be letting their kids do it because they think *you* know what is going on! To really be responsible, you have to face the peer pressure and talk to other parents—even if you think they may

MOTHERS:

Think of a time when your peers wanted you to let your daughter do something you decided not to go along with. Pick something you said no to because it was unsafe or not appropriate, not because you thought your daughter couldn't handle it.

• What made you decide you shouldn't do it?
• How did you manage not to do it?

DAUGHTERS:

Think of a time when you wanted to go along with a group of friends but decided you didn't agree with what they were doing.

• What made you decide you shouldn't do it?
• How did you manage not to do it?

Good for both of you for sticking up for yourselves!

see you as silly or nosy or distrustful. If you don't, you may end up backing down completely on something you think could be harmful or wrong, and your daughter will be forced to make the decision on her own.

Preventing Problems

EVEN THOUGH a mother does her best to make sure situations are safe for her daughter, she feels better when she knows she is able to stand up to peer pressure. Daughters, you may not know how to reassure your mother that you can handle difficult situations. Here are some things that may help:

- *Talk about your life.* The best way to show your mother you are comfortable in peer situations is to tell her about the things that go on around you. Instead of waiting for her to ask questions, tell her about the pressure some of your peers put on you or your friends. Talking about these things doesn't mean you are going to do them. Your mother will be pleased to know that you are aware of them. Be sure to tell her about times you stay away from situations where peers could pressure you and times when you stick up for yourself. It will help her see that you don't do things just because your peers want you to do them.

- *Get educated.* Another way to show your mother that you can handle yourself is to learn about the things that *could* happen. If you know what others might want you to do, you won't be completely surprised if they ask. They could want you to skip school or not do your homework. They could want you to lie, cheat, or take drugs that change the way your mind and body work. They could want to touch you in ways that make you uncomfortable. They could encourage you to shoplift or join a gang. You can learn more about these situations by talking to your mother, watching educational programs, or going to community classes together when they are offered.

- *Know your friends.* Both mothers and daughters do better at facing peer pressure if they stick with people they know feel the same way they do, or at least won't pressure them to be different. Talk to your friends about some of the situations you could face and find out what they would do. Try to hang around people who feel the same way you do.

Talk about situations that would make you uncomfortable. Discuss the reasons other people might want you to do certain things. And talk about what could happen if you did them. With your friends, think of ways you could help each other out of a tough situation.

- *Be ready.* It can be hard to think of responses to peers when they are standing there pressuring you to do something. If you plan a few responses ahead of time, you won't have to come up with them on the spot. Here are some simple things you can practice before you get into a situation where someone says, "Aw, come on."

1. *Ignore them.* There are several ways to do this. You can act like you didn't hear them. Or you can change the subject. Or you can simply walk away.

2. *Say no.* There are many ways to say no. The simplest is to say the word clearly and with confidence, looking the person in the eyes. Milder ways to say it are: "I don't want to," "Not today," or "I already have plans." If they keep at you, say it again. And keep saying it until they stop—even if they make fun of you.

3. *Look around for support.* In any given situation, there is a good chance someone else is as uncomfortable as you are and would appreciate your speaking up. Invite that person to go with you to do something else. Realize that standing up for what you believe may get you more respect than going along with something you don't want to do. It might make others who feel pressured to do it feel a lot more comfortable, too.

4. *Use your parents as an excuse.* If "I can't" or "I don't want to" doesn't work, try, "My parents will ground me," or even "My mother's really mean." (Ask your mom if she'd

rather you said something like that than do something you thought was wrong!)

What's a Mother to Do?

JUST BECAUSE daughters become more influenced by peers as they grow up does not mean their mothers become unimportant to them. Mothers still give strong messages about how to behave as a grown-up and as a woman. They continue to be role models by what they do and say. Here are a few things mothers can do to help their daughters get through the transition to adulthood.

1. *Set an example of standing up to peer pressure.* Show your daughter that you don't do what people want you to do without thinking it through. Talk to her about situations you run into and how you stood up to your peers.

2. *Talk to your daughter about situations you see going on.* Mention situations you have heard are going on at your daughter's school or in the neighborhood that you think could involve peer pressure. This doesn't mean being a gossip. You can talk about situations without assuming that they are true or including names. Invite your daughter to discuss what she would do if the situation ever came up, and don't be too quick to tell her what you think is right. Let her know you are genuinely interested in what she thinks. Make sure she feels it is okay to be uncertain in her beliefs when she talks to you. Be sympathetic about her fears of peer rejection or ridicule.

3. *Try to know your daughter's friends.* Have them over to your house. Go to events in which your daughter is involved, and meet the people she knows. Be active with

MOTHERS AND DAUGHTERS:

Talk about how you would handle the following problem situations. What would you do? What would you say? How would you say it? What ways might the other person react? How would you handle their reaction?

FOR MOTHERS:

- Your friend wants to take her daughter and yours to a movie you haven't seen, but it is rated R.
- A friend wants to drive you home and you know she has been drinking a lot of alcohol.

FOR DAUGHTERS:

- A friend offers you a cigarette.
- You are in a store with a group of friends. One of them drops an item off the shelf into her purse. She tells you to do the same thing.

her, if you can, in group activities and organizations she finds interesting.

4. *Talk directly to adults who know your daughter.* Visit with teachers, parents, and other adults that know and influence your daughter and her peers. It can help you to know the situations she faces.

MOTHERS AND DAUGHTERS:

- Talk about something you saw someone do
  that you disagree with. Did he or she try to
  get you to do the same thing? What would
  you do if they did?

- Talk about a time you were not sure what to
  do because someone important to you was
  pressuring you. How did you handle it?

5. *Negotiate with your daughter about rules.* You make the rules, but it doesn't hurt to listen to your daughter's point of view. Let her know that you understand what she is thinking and feeling even when you disagree with her. Then do what you think is right. (Chapter 8 talks about how to negotiate with each other.)

6. *Set limits.* You aren't always going to allow the same activities or privileges other parents do. Be comfortable with your own rules and standards, and don't be afraid to call other parents. When there are limits that are important to you, be clear and consistent with your daughter.

7. *Intervene when necessary.* When you have a sense that certain people aren't good for your daughter, you are the one who must decide whether to limit their time together. Teachers and other leaders can be a good source of information, but most of them will not try to influence friendships. You will need to decide when to draw the line on a relationship. Try not to make the mistake of breaking up a friendship

just because the friend *looks* different. What really counts is how the friend behaves and whether her behavior is likely to get your daughter into trouble. If you hear that one of her friends is doing things you don't like, remember that your daughter might not agree with it, either. She may already have stood up to pressure to do the same thing. Find out by talking with her about it.

Are You Mad at Me?

BECAUSE MOST GROUPS of friends are growing up around the same time, friendships can get pretty complicated. Everybody is trying to figure out who she is and who she wants to become. When people go through changes, they need someone to talk to and confide in. But sometimes it is hard to tell who you can trust to listen and help you. Even your best friend can make you feel not so good about yourself. You may get mad at each other. Sometimes you may not speak for days. Your mother can't fix these things for you, and you would not want her to get involved in some situations anyway. But she may be able to offer some useful suggestions if

---

MOTHERS AND DAUGHTERS:

Talk about a time when:

• You felt left out of a group or an activity.
• A good friend turned against you.

How did these situations turn out?

---

you explain what is going on and ask for her ideas. It can help just to talk about these things with someone who loves you and wants to listen.

Mothers, if your daughter comes to you about a problem with her friends, be sure she is asking for advice before you give it. She may just want you to understand how she is feeling, and it may help her to talk about the problem out loud. If she is looking for suggestions, tell her what has worked for you in the past, but try not to expect her to handle the situation in the same way you would. She isn't you. Even if she shoots down your ideas, hearing you talk about them may help her come up with her own solutions. She may need just your listening and understanding, not your advice.

Daughters, remember that when friends are mean it can have as much to do with how they are feeling at the moment as it does with anything you have done. Often their annoyance with you will pass when they get out of their mood. And a lot of times they will stop the way they are acting if you just don't react strongly to it. Other times, though, you may have to do something about it. Try telling your friend how you feel, and ask her to treat you differently. If she doesn't treat you better, try not to be mean back at her. Just concentrate on your other friends for a while. If that is hard to do because your friends are always with her, try inviting one of them to know you better by doing something separate from the group. Go to a movie or shopping, or just get together at your house for the afternoon. Do what *you* like to do. You may be surprised how much the friends you get to know this way like doing the same things you do.

When Others Tease You

I SAW AN EMBARRASSING situation once. A high school boy was dressed in his graduation cap and gown, waiting to receive his diploma. When they called his name, he walked proudly toward the stage, then tripped on the second step! Everyone in the audience laughed. Many people would have been embarrassed in that situation, but he turned confidently toward the audience and took a bow! I admired his poise. After the ceremony, I heard many kids tease him about being a klutz, but he laughed with them and seemed to enjoy the attention. He turned an embarrassing situation into a joke about himself, and everyone liked him for it.

Being teased can be frustrating or fun, depending on why other people do it. Sometimes they are mean and want you to be bothered by it. Other times they like you and think they are being funny. It can be hard to tell the difference. Telling them you don't like being teased might work. But if you do that in front of other people, it often causes them to tease you more. It is usually best to assume that the people teasing you are doing it because they like you and to laugh right along with them. Then you won't seem so easy to fluster and fun to tease. If they are really cruel with name-calling or pranks, it might be worth asking an adult to be within earshot the next time. That way it won't look like you tattled on them.

For good-natured teasing, going along with the joke can show that you are a good sport. It puts others at ease and gives them a reason to like you. I am five feet tall—average height for a twelve-year-old. But I wasn't this tall when I was twelve. In fact, I have never been as tall as other people my age. And needless to say, I took a lot of teasing for it. "Hey, stand up!"—when I was standing up. "How's it feel to be the last one to know when it's raining?" "Small world, isn't it?" It didn't really matter why they teased me—I didn't let any of it bother me. I learned to laugh right along with them.

One of my clients, Carrie, was being teased on the school bus. For months she was the only one who got on at her stop. But then a new boy moved into her neighborhood.

When they got on the bus together, the kids giggled and made kissing noises at her. One of the boys hollered, "Hey, when's the wedding?" Carrie was horribly embarrassed. She needed time to rethink and plan a way to look less bothered by the situation. We made a plan. The next time it happened, Carrie was ready with a comeback. "When's the wedding?" the boy chided. "The day after yours," she answered, laughing. Everyone else laughed, too. Going along with the joke stopped the teasing. It just wasn't worth doing anymore.

Carrie chose a comeback that wasn't cruel for a response. If she had gotten angry and called the boy a name, it would have made things worse. She found a good-natured way to look like she thought the boy's joke was funny and stop him from teasing her more. Other things she could have said are:

- I wouldn't want to make you jealous.
- *You're* more my type.
- We're waiting till we finish middle school.

MOTHERS AND DAUGHTERS:

- Talk about a time you thought someone got too bothered by teasing, which made others tease her more.
- Talk about a time you saw someone handle teasing well.
- Invent a comeback to someone who teases you about a new haircut. Be sure not to be cruel to the other person.

Handling Rumors

AT SOME POINT in your life someone will say something about you that isn't true. She will tell someone else, who will tell someone else, and a rumor will go around. When I was a teenager, I took driver's education. The first day we drove, the instructor put us in a huge car I could barely see out of. When it was my turn to drive, I checked the mirrors and backed very slowly into a post! There was no damage to the car or the post, but by the end of the day rumors were everywhere. According to some people, I had run a red light, stopped in an intersection, and caused a huge accident. According to others, I had been taken away in a police car!

Needless to say, this was a very embarrassing situation, and it posed an interesting dilemma. When rumors fly, you can easily make the situation worse by the way you react. If you get angry and try too hard to defend yourself, you might make others think the rumors are true. You might want to talk over how to handle such a situation with your mother. There are several things you can do besides growing up and writing a book to tell what really happened. Here are some approaches you can take to help things die down:

- Stay calm and appear unbothered by the situation. Remember, the rumor is just talk to everyone else. They have no way of knowing if it is true or not. They are going to watch your reaction to see if you look ashamed or guilty.

- Try to see the rumor for what it is—ridiculous. It may even be funny if you can manage not to take it too seriously.

- Tell two or three friends that the rumor isn't true. Let them tell other people the facts rather than doing all the defending yourself.

- Don't turn around and start a rumor about someone else. That will just make the other person angry and more likely to tell other stories about you.
- Forget it as soon as possible. Everyone else will.

Sometimes people don't mean to start rumors. Other times they do it on purpose. If the person starting a hurtful rumor is someone you thought was a friend, you might want to look at how it happened and examine your friendship a little closer. If this person does the following things a lot of the time, you may want to look elsewhere for friends. Does he or she:

- make you feel uncomfortable about yourself?
- make fun of you?

MOTHERS AND DAUGHTERS:

What do you like about your friends? Here are several qualities both mothers and daughters tell me are important to them. Add others that aren't on the list. Pick the five that are most important to you. Tell each other why you chose the ones you did.

- Listens to me
- Tells the truth
- Does what she says she will do
- Can keep a secret
- Cares about me
- Talks to me
- Is fun
- Doesn't spread rumors
- Treats other people well

- do things to other people that make you uncomfortable?

- make you worry whether he or she will be your friend the next day?

- push you to do things you think are wrong?

A Matter of Trust

BEING A GOOD FRIEND always involves trust. You need to believe that you will care about each other, tell the truth to each other, and keep each other's secrets. Not revealing the private thoughts and feelings your friend has shared with you to anyone else is one of the best qualities you can have as a friend, especially if you want her to treat you the same way. Not giving away the secret of a surprise party or a birthday present is fun. Writing secret notes to each other can be exciting. And it may be important not to tell others that your friend likes a certain boy or has a secret fear of horseback riding. Most secrets don't hurt anybody and can make a friendship more meaningful. But there are a few secrets that aren't good to keep—even for a friend.

Suppose your best friend told you that someone was hurting her. You would not want that to continue even if she told you not to tell anyone, that she would not be your friend if you told. If she could stop that person from hurting her, she obviously would have. You won't be able to stop it, either, unless you tell someone. There are other secrets like that, too. When I was a girl one of my friends often said she was going to run away. She said it to a lot of people, but nobody believed her. One night she told me she was really going to do it and not to tell on her. She left through her upstairs window. I thought about it for a while and then I told her parents. They were glad I did. The police found her and brought her back safely. I probably should have told

---

MOTHERS AND DAUGHTERS:

• What other situations can you think of where it might be best to tell an adult about something a friend is doing or planning to do? (If you disagree about some situations, that's fine. Just be sure to listen to each other's reasons and tell each other how you feel. Don't worry about convincing each other of your point of view right now. The situation may never come up! But this way you will know how the other person feels.)

• Name some adults you could you talk to if your mother wasn't nearby.

---

someone sooner, but I was trying to be a good friend by keeping a secret. I was glad I told them before it was too late. It was not safe for her to be out at that time of night by herself. My friend was mad at me only for a little while before she realized that I had told her secret because I cared about her and did not want her to get hurt.

It doesn't feel good to tell on a friend—especially when you know she will be angry that you did. But it is a good kind of tattling if you are telling someone so your friend can get help. If you are unsure whether to tell, ask your mother if *she* would want to know if this was *your* secret, and what she would do about it. If she says she would want to know, there is a good chance your friend's family would feel the same way. Tell your mother or another responsible adult about anyone you think may be in danger.

CHAPTER 8

How to Get (at Least Some of)
What You Want from Each Other

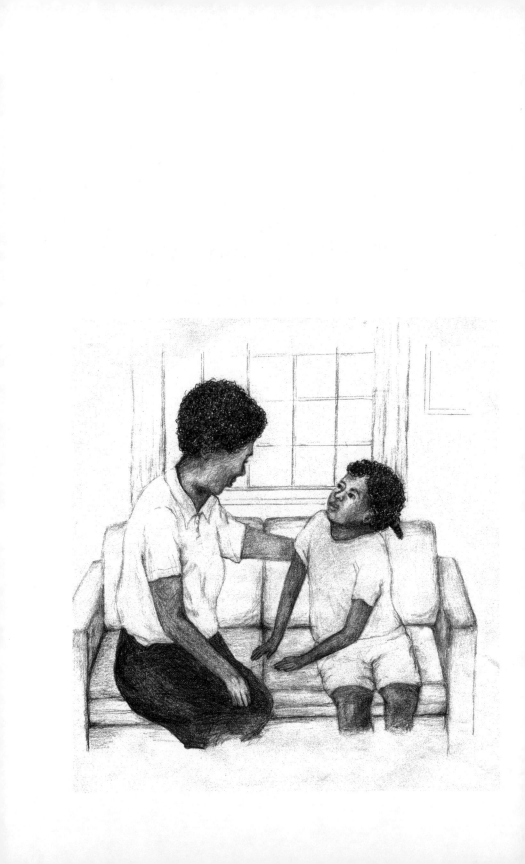

PRETEND FOR A minute that you just finished swimming at your neighborhood pool. You and your friends leave the building without getting your hands stamped because you don't plan to return. A few minutes later you realize that you left your purse inside. When you try to enter the pool again, a lifeguard blocks your way. She just took over at the desk and doesn't recognize you. She wants you to pay to go in again. What do you do?

- Call the lifeguard a name?
- Make a nasty remark about her to one of
  your friends?
- Push her out of the way?
- Hit her?

I hope you wouldn't do any of these things! They would be rude, not to mention a waste of time. None of them would get you back into the pool to get your purse. Some of them could even get you in trouble. When you were younger you might have cried in a situation like this, or waited for your mother to talk to the lifeguard. But the older you get, the more you will find yourself in situations where *you* have to take care of disagreements with people. You are better able to reason with them now and to understand what they are thinking. But you have to be careful not to let your feelings get in the way.

When others disagree with us, it is easy to feel that neither we nor our feelings matter to them. We may even think they are deliberately trying to make things difficult for us. These things may or may not be true. But if we think that they are true without checking those thoughts against reality, we act as though the things *are* true. When that lifeguard blocks your way and tells you that you have to pay again, you might feel she doesn't understand you or care about you. But showing your anger or frustration would probably not make her care more about you. In fact, it might make her angry, too. Then she *certainly* wouldn't help you. If you acted rude, you would get even less of what you wanted from her. You might even get kicked out of the pool for the summer. Your friends might feel embarrassed by your behavior and want to get away from you, or they might get frustrated and join in the fight. Little disagreements have a way of getting bigger and bigger.

Becoming a Good Salesperson

To GET PEOPLE to do what you want them to do, you have to be good salesperson. That notion might seem a little odd, since you aren't trying to sell them a product. But you are trying to sell them an *idea*. You want them to see things your

> MOTHERS AND DAUGHTERS:
>
> Talk about a time you tried to sell something to someone else. What did you do to get them to "buy" your product or idea?

way and go along with what you want—the definition of a good salesperson.

Salespeople know that doing certain things will help them make a sale. Some of them even go to school to learn how to do it. You probably have used some of the same techniques yourself to help people see things your way. Here are five essential steps to making a sale:

1. *Be sure the other person understands what you want from her.* Sometimes we think others should understand our position without being told what it is. But they can't know exactly what we need unless we tell them. The lifeguard in our example would not know you had just been in the pool. Most people who come to her desk either pay to get in or have a stamp on their hand telling her they have already paid. You may have to explain patiently that you just left the pool, you didn't plan to come back, but you need to get your purse. To make sure she has heard you correctly, you may need to repeat your story again. Be patient with this part. I have seen many arguments get worse because one person got angry with another person for making her repeat something several times.

2. *Stay calm.* It is wise not to act angry right away if it looks like the other person is not going to give you what you want. It will only make her angry in return. But staying calm may take some practice. Try taking a deep breath, counting to ten, or thinking about something else for a minute. If you get angry rather than listening to the other person, you will ruin your chance to sell your idea.

3. *Try to think what the other person's concerns might be.* If you can think of the reasons the other person might not want to do what you want, you can be ready with an answer —or even take care of her concerns before she tells you about them. Say, "I thought you might be worried that I was trying to sneak into the pool, so I ___."

4. *Listen to the other person's concerns and ask her to explain.* The other person may not be as good as you are at saying what her concerns are, or she might rattle off a whole list. Either way, it is a good idea to listen to what she has to say. She may have important concerns and you may have a way to take care of them. Suppose the lifeguard has had trouble with kids sneaking into the pool? Suppose she is afraid of getting into trouble with her boss if she lets you in? If she gets angry when you try to reenter the pool, find out why. If she says, "You're just like those kids that sneaked in last week," you might be able to help her see that your situation is different.

5. *Be ready to compromise.* If you get creative with your thinking, you might come up with a way you could *both* get what you want or need. With the lifeguard, you might think of several ways to reassure her that you are not trying to sneak into the pool besides just telling her that. You could describe your purse to her. You could leave her with something of value to you to prove that you are coming right back. Maybe she could go with you to get your purse. Maybe she could have someone look for it for you. Your initial idea of walking right back in to get your purse may not work in this situation. You might have to compromise.

Mothers and Daughters as Salespeople

MOTHERS AND daughters often run into situations where one of them wants something from the other. Daughters may want permission to go somewhere, money to spend, or help in doing a project. Mothers may want their daughters to do chores, finish homework, or stop doing something annoying. Parents, of course, have the final say, and daughters have to do some things just because they are told to do them. But all of us feel more cared about if our side of an issue is heard before a decision is made. Unless a parent says the topic is

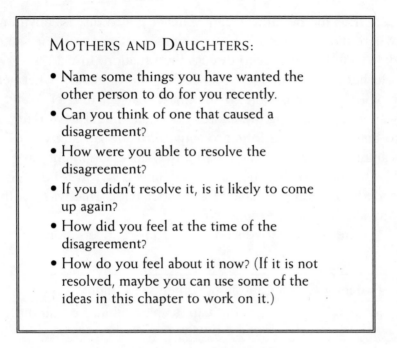

MOTHERS AND DAUGHTERS:

- Name some things you have wanted the other person to do for you recently.
- Can you think of one that caused a disagreement?
- How were you able to resolve the disagreement?
- If you didn't resolve it, is it likely to come up again?
- How did you feel at the time of the disagreement?
- How do you feel about it now? (If it is not resolved, maybe you can use some of the ideas in this chapter to work on it.)

not open for discussion, it might be worth talking about it.

Here is an example of a daughter trying to sell her mother on the idea of having a friend come over one evening. Read their conversation and see if you can pick out where the daughter went wrong as a salesperson.

Daughter	Can Marty come over tonight?
Mother	I'd rather not tonight.
Daughter	You never let me do what I want to do!
Mother	That isn't true.
Daughter	*Leaves the room. Slams door.*
Mother	*Calls after her:* You're grounded, young lady. I could use some help around here now and then, you know.

This mother and daughter never got to discuss anything. Where did the daughter go wrong as a salesperson? First, she didn't ask her mother to discuss the situation. Instead, she told her how mean she was. Second, she didn't ask what her mother's concerns were. If she knew that her mother really wanted help getting the chores done, she might have offered to help. Finally, she forgot to stay calm. She got angry and slammed her door. That ended any chance she might have had to convince her mother to do things her way. She even ended up getting punished for her behavior. That was not the way she had hoped things would go!

Here is another version of the same conversation:

Daughter	Can Marty come over tonight?
Mother	No, you want to play while I do all the work. No way.
Daughter	That's not fair.
Mother	Don't tell me what's fair, young lady. Now go to your room.

This time the mother shut the discussion down before the daughter had a chance to suggest a compromise. She failed to sell her daughter on helping her with the chores. She didn't explain what she needed, and she didn't listen to her daughter. Again, neither of them got what she wanted.

On the next page is the same conversation with two good salespeople. Notice how each of them sells the other on her ideas. Each of them says what she wants, listens to the other person, and compromises on the solution. And each of them gets at least some of what she wants from the other person.

This daughter did not get everything she wanted from her

Daughter	Says what she wants	Can Marty come over tonight?
Mother	Answers	I'd rather not tonight.
Daughter	Asks to discuss it further	Can we discuss this a little? I was hoping to show her my new outfit.
Mother	Hears daughter's objections and says what she wants from her	That would be nice. But there is a lot of work to get done around here.
Daughter	Asks for her to explain	What do you need to get done?
Mother	Explains	I have all this laundry to do tonight and dishes to get done.
Daughter	Offers a compromise solution	What if I help you with them first?
Mother	Notices daughter's effort and explains further	That's nice of you. I can sure use the help. But I'd still rather not have another person around tonight. I was hoping to spend some time as a family.
Daughter	Stays calm and offers an alternative	Okay, if it has to be that way. What about later this week?
Mother	Agrees	Tomorrow night would be fine.

mother, but she got something close to it: She will be able to see her friend the next night. She managed to stay calm and not get into trouble for her behavior. The mother got some of what she wanted, too—help with the chores and a night to spend with the family. Because they were willing to negotiate and to respect each other's wishes, everybody ended up feeling cared about. This makes it more likely they will listen to each other the next time one of them makes a request.

MOTHERS AND DAUGHTERS:

• Think again of situations where one of you wanted something from the other. Try to act like good salespeople and talk about it again. Pretend it is happening right now and practice your selling and compromising skills with each other.

• Can you think of a time when you had to compromise to get some of what you wanted?

Deal Breakers

AS YOU SAW in these examples, certain behaviors can keep a salesperson from making a sale, like not being clear about a request or getting upset with the other person. Below are some other deal breakers to watch out for.

Blaming the Other Person. When we are angry we often decide that we know what the other person is thinking or feeling better than the other person does. We may feel she is rejecting us or trying to hurt us. In turn, we may blame her. But blaming the other person almost always stops a sale.

Notice how each blaming sentence starts with the word *you*. Saying *you* at the start of a sentence often makes it sound like you are blaming the other person, which makes that other person feel hurt or angry. Then she is likely to end the conversation without giving you what you want. Usually we blame someone else when we have strong feelings we aren't saying. When we tell the other person what those feelings are, we give her a chance to help us feel better. When those blaming *you* statements come to mind, stop. Think,

Don't . . .	Do . . .
Blame the other person.	Say how you feel.
By . . .	**By . . .**
Saying things like:	Saying things like:
"You hate me."	"I feel angry when . . . "
"You just don't care."	"I feel hurt that . . . "
"You made me do it."	"I'm afraid they'll make fun of me."

"What am I feeling?" Then tell the other person, starting your sentence with *I* instead of *you*.

Using "Closed" Body Language. Did you know that you say things to people without talking to them, just by the way you sit, stand, or hold your body? Waving can mean hello or good-bye. Turning your thumb up means "good job." Other gestures tell people we are open to hearing what they have to say, like smiling or leaning closer to them. And some say we are closed to listening, like turning our backs or holding our hands over our ears.

Exaggerating. When we are afraid that we aren't going to get something we want, it is easy to say things that are a little—or a lot—exaggerated. We try to make a point by telling people

Don't . . .	Do . . .
Use closed body language.	Use open body language.
By . . .	**By . . .**
Standing with your hands on your hips.	Keeping your arms at your sides or in front of you.
Pointing or shaking a finger.	Looking at the person while talking.
Glaring or rolling your eyes.	

MOTHERS AND DAUGHTERS:

- Describe some other body language that tells people you want to hear what they have to say.

- Describe some body language that tells people you don't want to listen, don't like what they are saying, or don't like them.

---

that things *always* happen a certain way or that *everybody* does a certain thing. We take something that has happened a few times and act like it happens all the time, just to convince others that it is true. Sometimes we even convince ourselves.

Other people get angry or irritated when we exaggerate. They know that most things don't happen all the time and that people aren't always a certain way. They know everybody doesn't do something, and they don't trust us if we exaggerate. They may even get angry about it.

Don't . . .	**Do . . .**
Make broad, general statements.	Be specific about the situation.
By . . .	**By . . .**
Saying things like:	Saying things like:
"You *always* say that."	"Tell me what you are concerned about."
"I *never* get to do anything."	"I would like to go this time; it's really important to me."
"*Everybody's* going."	"Some of my friends are going and I'd really like to be with them."

Don't . . .	**Do . . .**
Bring up old arguments.	Stay on the topic.
Talk about other people's situations.	Talk about *your* situation.
By . . .	**By . . .**
Getting off track.	Saying:
Saying things like:	"Here's what I'd like to do."
"You were late yesterday."	"Let's talk about how we can
"You let Sara do it last year."	work this situation out."
"You made a mistake last summer."	

Getting off the Track. When we argue with people, we try to get them to see things our way. One of the ways we do that is to talk about other situations we have been in. But sometimes those situations don't have much to do with what is going on now with us. We bring up things that happened a long time ago or involved other people, like how she snored last weekend or how your sister got to go to the zoo. Old arguments and other people's experiences only get the conversation off the track. You may notice that a lot of off-the-track statements start with the word *you* and also sound blaming.

Missing the Chance to Compromise. When it looks like the person we want something from is going to say no, it is easy to simply give up or get angry, or both. If we make the other person angry, she doesn't hear anything else we say. Everyone goes away frustrated, and we don't get what we wanted. To make matters worse, the other person will not be very anxious to listen to us the next time we make a request. We miss our chance to compromise. We might do better if we can offer some ideas about how we both get a little of what we want from each other.

Don't . . .	Do . . .
Miss the chance to compromise.	Try to compromise. Offer alternative solutions.
By . . .	**By . . .**
Doing other deal-breaking behaviors. Forgetting to offer other ideas.	Saying things like: "How can I make you feel better about this?" "Is there anything I can do to change your mind?" "What if I do this . . . ?"

Not Taking No for an Answer. Nobody likes to be told no. When you were little you might have screamed, cried, or whined in response. Now that you are older you don't do that as much; for one thing, it's a sure way to get into trouble. But you have to be careful not to stomp off or slam doors, because they get the same result.

If your parent says a discussion is over, accept it. Some things aren't negotiable and have to be done just because

Don't . . .	Do . . .
Expect to get exactly what you want.	Accept no as an answer if it is final. Increase your chances the next time around.
By . . .	
Thinking only you should have your way. Throwing a tantrum if it doesn't work out this time. Taking it as a personal put-down when you are told no.	**By . . .** Saying that you understand. Thinking about how to handle it next time. Understanding the concerns the other person has so you can offer solutions in the future.

MOTHERS AND DAUGHTERS:

• Just for fun, try using some deal breakers in the following situation where the daughter wants something from the mother. Remember that you are just pretending!

Daughter: Your mother wants your room cleaned before company comes an hour from now. You are busy writing letters and want to watch your favorite TV show in about five minutes.

Mother: Ask your daughter to clean her room. Say something like: "I'd like you to clean your room before our company gets here in an hour."

• How did you feel toward each other when you used deal breakers? Do you think either of you would get what you want behaving like this?

• Now try it again using what you have learned about being a good salesperson.

the parent says so. Be sure not to ask the other parent for a different answer. If you can be reasonable even if you are disappointed, you will increase your chances of making a sale the next time you want something.

What compromises did you come up with? Did either of you suggest cleaning only part of the room? Doing part of the room before the show and part afterward? Closing the door? Taping the television show? Asking for help? There are a lot of ways to get at least *some* of what you want.

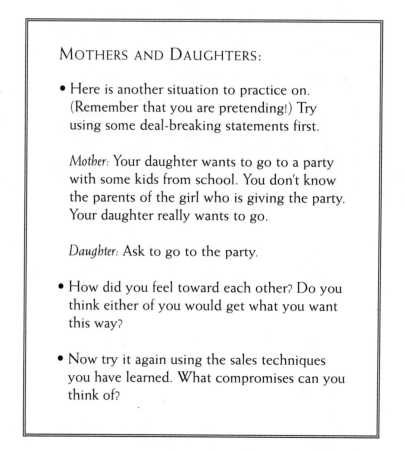

MOTHERS AND DAUGHTERS:

- Here is another situation to practice on. (Remember that you are pretending!) Try using some deal-breaking statements first.

  Mother: Your daughter wants to go to a party with some kids from school. You don't know the parents of the girl who is giving the party. Your daughter really wants to go.

  Daughter: Ask to go to the party.

- How did you feel toward each other? Do you think either of you would get what you want this way?

- Now try it again using the sales techniques you have learned. What compromises can you think of?

What to Do if Things Heat Up

SOMETIMES THE person we are talking to is grouchy and irritable and just seems to want to fight. It can happen with a brother or sister, a lifeguard, or even a mother or daughter. If the other person uses deal breakers a lot, we tend to do the same thing and often get into trouble. If we give up, the conversation ends without getting what we want. Trying to calm things down is usually a better idea.

The best way to calm another person down is to recognize how she is feeling. Letting her know you understand that she is angry or disappointed can help her stop wanting to fight. Many times there is something you can agree on—that you are both tired, that you actually want her to be able to go to the party, or that the room would look better if it is cleaned before five. If this doesn't work, it is probably worth suggesting that you discuss the issue another time. There is no reason to be treated rudely. Parents can and should discipline behaviors that are really out of line. But if you stop before the situation heats up, you have a better chance of reaching a compromise when you pick it up later.

If you decide to discuss things at another time, be sure to do it. Agree with each other that you will start the conversation over without being angry at each other. Sometimes arguments are even a little funny when you look back at them. Talk about what each of you could have done differently. And do your best to leave out the deal breakers.

CHAPTER 9

Thinking Things Out

As YOU GROW UP, you will have more and more decisions to make about how to live your life. Some of them—such as whether to go to college, where to live, and what kind of job you want to do—will be very important. Your future will depend on how you solve these problems, but you will be ready to make these decisions when the time comes. And you will have plenty of choices about what to do and how to do it.

Whether you realize it or not, you are already preparing to make the big decisions in your life. You practice by making many smaller decisions every day, decisions that you didn't have to make when you were little. You decide what to wear, when to study, and who to call on the phone. You are the only one who can decide what to do when your parents are not around. You decide how to behave at school and at friends' houses. You decide how to handle peer pressure. You probably also decide how to spend your own money.

Your mother makes a lot of everyday decisions, too. Many of them are similar to the ones you are already making. Your mother decides what time to get up in the morning. She decides how to get everything done. And she makes decisions at work such as what to do first and what to say at meetings with her boss. No matter what age you are or how small a decision you have to make, you need a way to think things through. Most of the time you can arrive at solutions by quickly figuring them out in your head. Other times you may need a paper and pencil and a little more time.

MOTHERS AND DAUGHTERS:

- Give an example of a decision you made today.
- Tell about a decision you made last week.

Were the decisions you made big ones or little ones? Do you know how you went about making them? Chances are you have a way of thinking things through that comes pretty naturally to you—so naturally, in fact, that you don't pay much attention to it. Think for a minute about how you do it. If your way of making a decision includes these five problem-solving steps, you will be ready to tackle even the most difficult problem that comes along. The steps are: (1) Say or write the problem; (2) Consider how important the problem is; (3) Name all the possible solutions; (4) Pick the best solution; and (5) Learn from it.

1. Say the Problem or Write It Down

IN ORDER TO make a good decision about something, you need to know exactly what the problem is. Otherwise you may choose a solution that doesn't make the situation better. In some situations, you know right away what is wrong: For

example, you forgot to take your homework assignment to
school or you have run out of gas on the highway. In one
case, the problem is that you need your homework to get
credit for doing it, but your homework is at your house. In
the other case you need gasoline to make your car move, but
the gas station is miles down the road. Even if you aren't sure
what to do in these situations, there is no question what the
problem is.

Other problems aren't so easy to identify. This happens
most often when strong feelings are involved. Feeling angry,
frustrated, or upset can get in the way of thinking clearly
about a situation. For example, suppose you have a fight
with your friends at school and end up eating lunch alone.
No one sits with you on the bus. When you get home, angry
and upset, you start feeling that you must have a new outfit
for the next day and beg your mother to take you shopping.
As you are going out the door, one of your friends calls to
talk for a while. After you speak with her, you no longer care
about going shopping. Maybe the problem wasn't that you
needed more clothes. Maybe you were just feeling lonely.

When you are faced with a situation that upsets you,
try saying what you think the problem is. Say it to yourself
or to a friend, but repeat it at least three times. Change how
you say it each time to see if there is a better way. Or write
it down several different ways. You may be surprised how a
problem becomes clearer when it is repeated and reworded.
One girl I worked with came to a therapy session very upset
one day. When I asked her what was wrong, she went
through the following rewording of her problem without my
ever saying a word!

*I want to run away from home, but I don't
have any money. No, I need to get away from my
parents, but I have nowhere to go. No, I want my*

parents to listen to me, but I don't know how to get them to do that.

This girl took several tries before she got to the real problem. Simply saying the problem out loud helped her figure out what it was. She also had another thing going for her. She worded her problem by saying what her goal was and what she thought was keeping her from it. Notice how each of her sentences started with the words *I need* or *I want.* Saying or writing what you want or need is the first part of identifying the problem. The second part is to say what is keeping you from reaching your goal. Problems that are clearly stated often end up being a sentence like this: "I want (or need)_____, *but* _____ is blocking my way." So, in my earlier example, the problem was not "I just have to buy a new outfit." It was "I want to talk to my friends, but I think they are all angry with me."

MOTHERS AND DAUGHTERS:

Complete this sentence for the decisions you said you made yesterday or last week.

"I wanted (or needed) _____, but _____."

---

2. *Consider How Important the Problem Is*

BEFORE YOU SPEND a lot of time searching for the solution to a problem, you will want to think about how important it is. That way you will know whether it is worth the time and energy you have to put into solving it. There are several questions to ask yourself in this step, including: How big is the problem? How much of your life does it affect? Who else does it affect? And when do you have to decide?

How Big Is the Problem? Sometimes little problems seem like big ones. It is easy to worry about things we have little control over, like whether the ball game will get rained out or whether the bus will be on time. And it is easy to get emotional about things that seem different or unfamiliar, like whether we will make any friends at a new camp or whether we will like our new teacher. The best we can do is keep a level head and try to prepare for such situations. There may be things you can do to make a situation more bearable even if the worst happens. If you get angry or upset ahead of time, you will convince yourself the situation is hopeless, and you will indeed have a bad time. Or you will have stayed up all night worrying about what could happen and be too tired to enjoy what does.

How Much of Your Life Does It Affect? One reason some problems seem more important than they are is that we forget they affect only a small part of our lives. A ball game getting rained out may matter that particular day but won't matter next week, and certainly won't next year. Getting the teacher you didn't want will affect only nine months of a year, not your whole school career. To put things in perspective, look at the spot on the line below. It represents a single day out of a whole year made up of 365 days.

Today	The Rest of the Year

Now imagine this whole page filled with spots of that size. That's as big as today is in comparison with the rest of your life. Some things just don't affect your life as much as you might think they do at first. Ask yourself if the problem you face really matters a lot. What is the worst that can happen? Would it really be that bad? Will it matter tomorrow? Next week? Next year?

Who Else Does It Affect? Most of the time we make decisions that don't involve a lot of other people. But problems that involve other people can be very difficult. You have to weigh the feelings of others against your own, and what they want against what you think is right. For example, if you need to tell someone's secret in order to keep her from hurting herself, it is definitely worth letting her be angry with you for a little while. You don't want to hurt her feelings, but you don't want to make the wrong decision, either. You don't want to do something just because you think someone will be upset with you if you don't. Remember what was said earlier about peer pressure, and remember that everyone has ups and downs. What seems important to your friends one minute may not be as important to them the next. Consider all the possibilities, but make the decision that is right for you.

When Do You Have to Decide? One of the ways to know how important a problem is is to ask yourself what

MOTHERS AND DAUGHTERS:

You already named several decisions you made recently. Answer these questions about one of them:

- How big did you think the problem was?
- How much of your life did you think it would affect?
- Did it affect anyone else?
- Did you have to decide on a solution when you did?
- What would have happened if you hadn't made a decision?

would happen if you did nothing at all. Suppose you have three days off from school when you can do anything you want to do. If you don't make a decision about what to do, your time off will probably not turn out the way you want it to. You have a problem worth solving: You need to decide how to spend your time. Do you want to do something fun? Do you want to involve other people? There are a lot of activities to choose from. You could ride your bike or go shopping or clean your room (okay, probably not, huh?). But if you don't make a choice, you will be deciding not to do anything at all! Is there a deadline? If there is, why wait? The sooner you figure this one out, the more time you will have to do it! Some decisions have to be made quickly or it is too late.

3. List All Possible Solutions

AFTER YOU HAVE decided how important a problem is and how quickly you have to make a decision, start thinking of solutions. Sometimes the first solution that pops into your mind isn't the best one. In fact, if you choose it right off, it will keep you from thinking of other, perhaps better ideas. Think back to the problem of forgetting your homework. If your first solution is to walk home and get it, and you immediately do that, you might not remember that your mother is coming to your school for a meeting and could bring it to you. You might not consider that your teacher might understand the situation if you told him or her what happened. And you might walk home unnecessarily. Think of all solutions before you jump to the one that seems most obvious to start with.

The best way to be sure you think of *every* possible solution is to write down *every* idea that comes into your head, no matter how silly it seems. This is called brainstorming, and the key to doing it is not to criticize any ideas right away. A silly idea may lead you to think of a not so silly idea you didn't think of to start with. Don't eliminate any ideas; just write them down as fast as you can think of them. You want to get every idea out there so you can choose the best one.

Another way to brainstorm is to do it with someone else. Two heads are often better than one. Agree with someone else that no idea will be considered foolish. Then take turns giving solutions without commenting on or criticizing them until you have no further thoughts. No one should say an idea is silly or won't work. Getting suggestions from someone else doesn't mean you have to follow them. And you just may hear some that you didn't think of yourself.

Your mother is a good person to brainstorm with. She will be glad you are thinking things through. Just be sure she knows that you are brainstorming and not asking what she thinks you should do. If she knows you are just gathering ideas, she will be careful not to criticize them as they come up or to give more weight to some ideas than others. And she won't be offended if you don't do what she says. Both of you will have fun with brainstorming.

One final note about brainstorming: Be sure to practice it with your friends. I talk to a lot of girls who say they are the one everybody comes to for help with problems. Often they have good problem-solving skills the others don't have,

---

MOTHERS AND DAUGHTERS:

- Name a decision you will need to make in the next week or so.
- Brainstorm with each other all possible solutions you can think of to the problem.
  (Be sure not to judge each other's ideas.)
- Write your list down.

---

and it makes them feel good that their opinions carry so much weight. But there are two things I tell them to watch out for. One is that if they give their friends the answer *they* think is best, their friends don't learn to solve problems on their own. The other is that when you are the problem solver, others can forget that you sometimes need their help with *your* decisions. If everybody knows how to brainstorm without giving their opinions right away or criticizing one another's ideas, you can all learn from one another.

4. Pick the Best Solution

WHEN YOU ARE ready to look at the solutions you brainstormed, you will probably see some you can get rid of right away. They may be silly or just not do-able. But there may be several you will want to consider. When you have trouble choosing the best one, it sometimes helps to say what you like and don't like about each one. Below is a chart I use to get all the possibilities out in front of me. I list every solution I am considering across the top. For each solution, I list the reasons I think it is good, then the reasons I think it is not.

Possible solutions	Solution 1	Solution 2	Solution 3
Reasons for doing this			
Reasons not to do this			

Here are some questions you might want to think about as you write reasons for and against your ideas:

- What will happen if I do it?
- Does it fit with my parents' views?
- Does it fit with my morals and my values?
- Does it fit with my goals?

Sometimes the right solution is not clear even after you list the reasons for and against each one. In this case you might want to get more detailed about the process. Try giving each solution a score. Give one point for every reason you came up with for that solution. Subtract a point for every reason you listed against it. Compare the totals you get for each solution. The one with the most points may be the best one, or you might decide that some reasons should get more points than others. It is totally up to you. At least you will know that you thought through all the possibilities and used your head to come up with the answer. The bottom line is, What do *you* think is the best thing to do?

On page 169 are some examples where I used the chart to consider several solutions to a problem. They include only a partial list of solutions. You can probably think of others.

MOTHERS AND DAUGHTERS:

- Make a chart like the one on page 167 for the decisions each of you said you have to make in the next few weeks. List all the solutions you brainstormed. Under each solution, list reasons for and against it. Give them scores if you want to.

- What do you think you should do in each of these situations?

Unfortunately, the answers to problems aren't usually black and white. The right solution isn't always obvious. If the solution to your problem isn't clear after you brainstorm and use the charts, it could be that your feelings are getting in the way. If there is a lot riding on the answer, you may find yourself having more trouble than usual. Use the skills

PROBLEM: I want to have Karen as a friend . . . but she is mad at me and saying bad things about me.

Possible solutions	Do nothing	Say bad things about her	Tell her mother	Ask her to stop
Reasons for doing this	She will probably be my friend again tomorrow.	I'll feel better.	She will make her stop.	She might stop. She might not know how bad I feel.
Reasons not to do this	She might keep it up.	She'll get madder at me.	She will be mad that I told, but she'll stop.	She might get worse. She'll know it bothers me.
What I think I should do	Wait a day and see what happens; if Karen is still mad at me, I'll ask her to stop. I'll think about telling her mother, but as a last resort.			

PROBLEM: I want to get good grades . . . but I don't understand the work and I am getting really far behind in my schoolwork.

Possible solutions	Do nothing	Study four hours every night	Cheat	Ask for help
Reasons for doing this	I don't know what to do.	I need to catch up.	I'll get better grades.	Someone could tutor me. Others have to have had this problem before.
Reasons not to do this	Things will only get worse.	No one can study that much. I know I won't really do it.	It is dishonest. I could get caught. I won't learn the material.	I'll have to do the work. I'll have to admit I'm failing.
What I think I should do	Ask my parents to help me find someone to tutor me in this subject.			

you learned earlier to identify your feelings. Ask yourself if you could be making assumptions without checking them out against reality. Talking to your mother about them may help. And sometimes, if you don't have an immediate deadline, it helps to just shelve your decision for a while. Get all your ideas on paper, then put the paper away for a day or two. The correct decision may be obvious when you look at the paper again.

5. *Learn from It*

THE FINAL STEP in problem-solving is to think about what you did and learn from it. Don't kick yourself if it didn't turn out the way you had intended. It is always easier to look back on a situation than it is to make a decision in the first place. The more you practice solving problems, the easier this activity will become. Think about the parts of the process that were helpful to you, and change the parts that weren't. No matter how it turned out, give yourself credit for working on the problem. You deserve a pat on the back for using a real problem-solving approach rather than jumping to the first or easiest solution. If the solution doesn't turn out like you wanted, just ask yourself what you could do differently the next time.

CHAPTER 10

Where Do We Go from Here?

WHAT ARE YOU going to be when you grow up? You've heard that question so many times! Even though adults ask it, they don't really expect you to have an answer right now, or even to know in the next several years. Most people change their mind five to ten times anyway, sometimes even when they are grown-ups. You will do a lot of thinking about your future while you are growing up. And the road to what you finally end up doing can be very interesting, indeed.

Many options will be open to you as you get older. You probably will have a job. You might go to college. And you might decide to have a family. Women have to decide what they need and want to do to take care of themselves and their families. Some women work in their homes taking care of their children. Some also work outside their home to earn money for the things their families need. However they spend their time, most women agree that it is best if they do things that interest them. They want to use their skills and talents doing something worthwhile, perhaps helping other people or the environment, and they are happiest when their activities excite or challenge them. When you grow up you will want to find work that you enjoy doing.

Part of deciding what to do as a grown-up involves figuring out who you are and what you like. That means trying new roles and activities. Even now, you wear your hair in different ways, try different outfits, and change how you speak to people to see how they react. You might have a hobby, play sports, or join the school chorus. You might try different ways of making a little money. Experimenting with any new role is a step toward your future—a step in discovering what you like to do and what you are good at.

MOTHERS AND DAUGHTERS:

- Tell about some ways you have changed how you look, speak, or act. How did people react?
- Name a few activities or hobbies you have tried. (Mothers, name some that you did at your daughter's age.) Which ones did you like?

Good Timing

YOU ARE LUCKY to be growing up today. In the past, women were given pretty strong messages about how they should run their lives. Sayings like "A woman's place is in the home" were common. Books, magazines, radio, and even comic books encouraged girls to be strictly homemakers. Men were supposed to go to work; women were to keep things in order at home. Most women grew up thinking they should not try to have a career. Many women who worked outside their homes worked in low-paying jobs as cashiers or typists. The few women who went to college usually became teachers or nurses, and their daughters were pretty much expected to do the same things when they grew up.

In the past, certain activities were considered "girl" activities or "boy" activities. There were definite differences in what girls and boys were supposed to be interested in. Boys were supposed to enjoy hobbies such as fishing, working on electrical equipment, building model airplanes, and carving wood. Girls were supposed to like needlecraft, cooking, and cake decorating. In school, girls were supposed to take home economics; boys, industrial arts. It was "sissy" stuff to cook or sew if you were a boy, and not good to like to saw or hammer if you were a girl. Today we see more girls and boys learning about hobbies and activities that they would have been laughed at in the past for trying.

Girls were treated differently than boys in school, too. In most schools, girls were required to wear dresses—no slacks. If they were allowed to wear pants, they certainly couldn't wear blue jeans. They were discouraged from calling boys on the phone; they were supposed to wait and hope to hear from them first. And organized sports like soccer, softball, and basketball were almost nonexistent for girls.

In the classroom, girls were not encouraged to learn math and science. After all, they weren't expected to go into mechanical or high-tech jobs, or even to go to college. Unfortunately, girls are often treated the same way today. Teachers don't call on them as often as they do boys. Sometimes girls act like they don't expect to be good at math or science, or pretend not to know the answers when they do. Girls don't raise their hands as much as boys do to answer math questions. These behaviors are carryovers from the way things used to be. But today women are working in jobs that require math and science skills more than ever before. And there are more jobs available to them when they know how to do these things. Being a girl does not mean you should stay away from math and science, or that you should keep quiet when you know the answers!

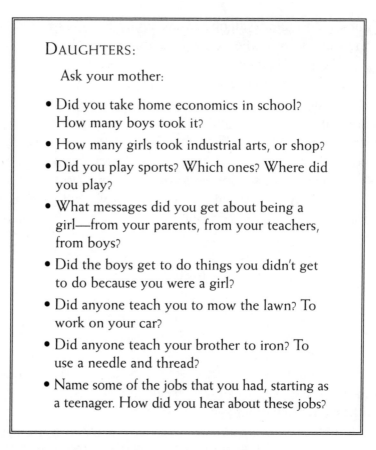

DAUGHTERS:

Ask your mother:

- Did you take home economics in school? How many boys took it?
- How many girls took industrial arts, or shop?
- Did you play sports? Which ones? Where did you play?
- What messages did you get about being a girl—from your parents, from your teachers, from boys?
- Did the boys get to do things you didn't get to do because you were a girl?
- Did anyone teach you to mow the lawn? To work on your car?
- Did anyone teach your brother to iron? To use a needle and thread?
- Name some of the jobs that you had, starting as a teenager. How did you hear about these jobs?

What Will You Be?

AS A YOUNG WOMAN today, you will have a lot of careers to choose from. Figure 5 lists a sampling of the many jobs that are out there. Next to each job is a line that shows how many women and men are doing that particular job. There are a lot more women than men in some occupations. Other occupations are almost exclusively male. This distribution could have something to do with what these people were encouraged or expected to do when they were kids.

I am certainly not suggesting that you should avoid any

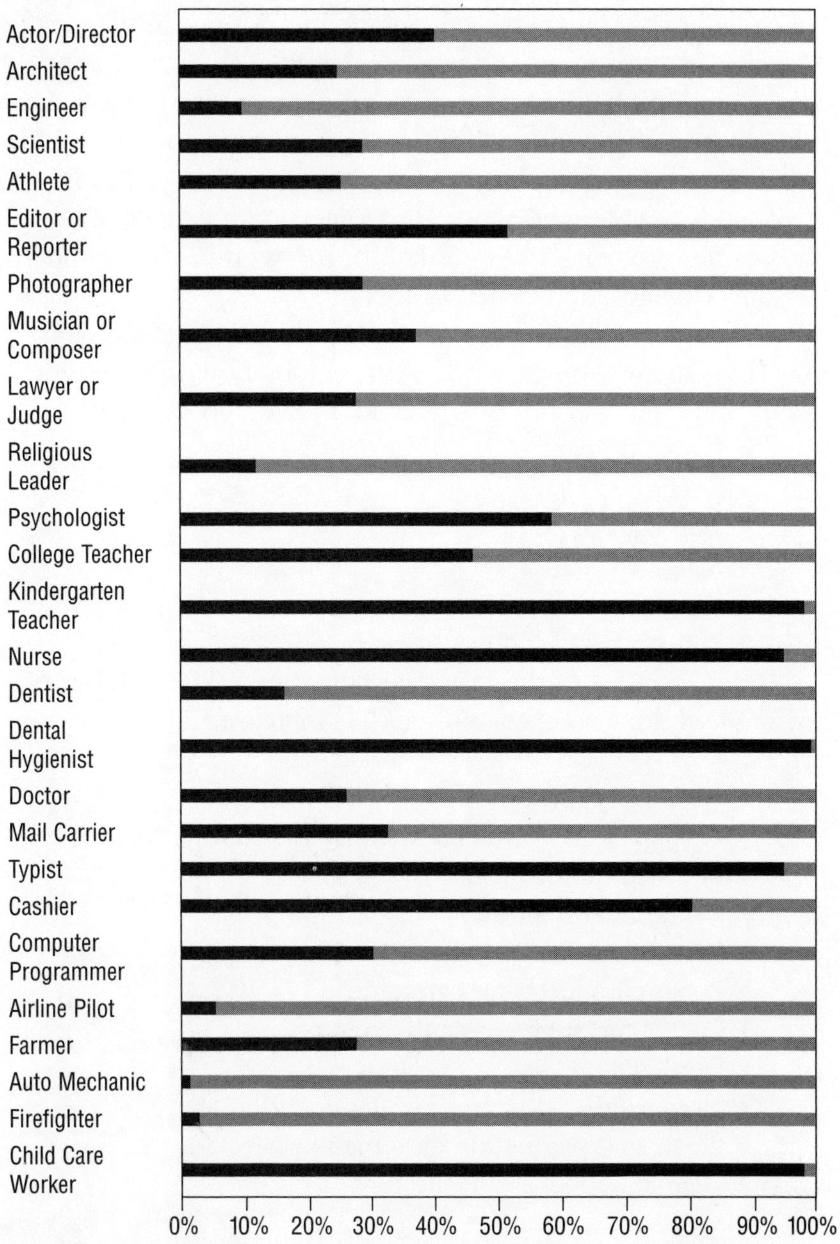

Figure 5. Males and females in different careers

■ Females
▨ Males

Data from: U.S. Bureau of the Census. Statistical Abstract of the United States: 1996 (116th edition). Washington, DC, 1996.

of the jobs that girls were encouraged to go into in the past.
A good job for you is one you like to do. I am just saying
that you don't have to become what anyone else thinks you
should be. And you don't have to stay away from things you
are interested in just because you are a girl. Today, almost
half of all people who work are women. Almost half of all
bosses are women. And over half of the workers in jobs that
require college degrees are women.

Here are some jobs more women are doing these days.
Twice as many women work in these jobs now than did ten
years ago—but still not nearly as many women as men.

- Police officer
- Firefighter
- Dentist
- Religious leader
- Farmer
- Foresters and loggers

Here is a list of the fastest-growing jobs. The number of
women working in each of them has increased in the last ten
years.

- Systems analyst
- Physical and corrective therapy assistant and aide
- Physical therapist
- Home health aide
- Human services worker
- Personal and home care aide
- Computer engineers and scientist
- Paralegal
- Occupational therapy assistants and aide
- Electronic pagination systems worker
- Teacher, special education
- Medical assistant
- Detective
- Correction officer
- Child care worker

How to Get There from Here

IT WILL BE A LONG time before you need to decide about careers. But it never hurts to look at your options, even at your age. Believe it or not, there are some things you can do right now to help yourself get ahead no matter what you decide to do later.

1. *Do your schoolwork.* The subjects you are taught in school may seem boring and unimportant at times. But you might be surprised to know that math, reading, and writing skills are used in almost every job you can think of. Here are a just a few examples of how different workers use these skills.

	Mathematics	Reading	Writing
Firefighter	Calculates oxygen in air masks	Reads labels on hazardous chemicals	Writes reports about what she did
Child care worker	Measures baby formula	Reads instructions left by parents	Writes reports about how child's day went
Dental hygienist	Times X rays	Reads setting on equipment	Writes results of examinations
Auto mechanic	Measures engine compression	Reads tables listing auto parts	Writes findings and charges
Doctor	Understands results of medical tests	Reads about how to treat diseases	Writes prescriptions and results of physicals

2. *Know yourself.* Finding a job that suits you means you have to know a lot about yourself. Here is a list of questions to help you think about your interests. If you think about the things you like to do and the way other people describe you, you can sometimes imagine yourself doing a certain kind of job.

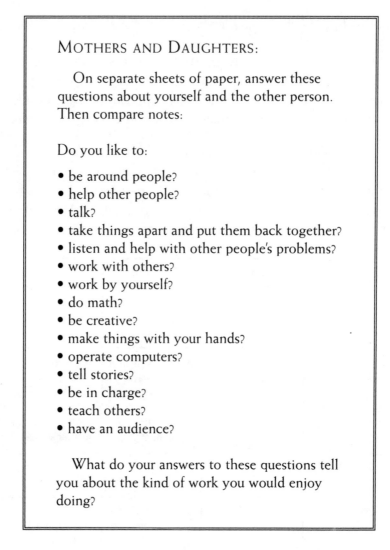

MOTHERS AND DAUGHTERS:

On separate sheets of paper, answer these questions about yourself and the other person. Then compare notes:

Do you like to:

- be around people?
- help other people?
- talk?
- take things apart and put them back together?
- listen and help with other people's problems?
- work with others?
- work by yourself?
- do math?
- be creative?
- make things with your hands?
- operate computers?
- tell stories?
- be in charge?
- teach others?
- have an audience?

What do your answers to these questions tell you about the kind of work you would enjoy doing?

As you learn about careers, think about which ones would benefit from the kind of skills and interests you have. And ask teachers and friends' parents who know you what careers they think you might enjoy.

3. *Find hobbies in your interest areas.* Another way to explore what you might like to do is through hobbies. Hobbies usually involve collecting, making, or discovering something.

They can teach you more than you are likely to learn in school about a particular topic and help you to gain new skills. (Hobbies also help other people know what to get you for birthdays and holidays!)

MOTHERS AND DAUGHTERS:

- Look at the list of hobby ideas below.
- Which ones have you tried?
- Which ones would you be interested in learning more about?
- What other hobbies can you think of?

Fishing
Bike riding
Cross-stitch
Swimming
Using computers
Model railroading
Sewing
Tying flies for fishing
Doing jigsaw puzzles
Research
Caring for a dog or cat
Taking apart electrical
  equipment
Collecting clocks
  or watches
Rug-making
Making friendship
  bracelets
Beekeeping
Archery
Picture-framing
Writing stories
Calligraphy
Painting
Ham radio operation

Hunting
Ceramics
Knitting
Collecting stamps,
  rocks, coins
Making doll clothes
Cake decorating
Inventing
Baby-sitting
Handicrafts
Carving
Model-making
Flower arranging
Jewelry-making
Candle-making
Cooking
Weaving
Painting
Lamp-making
Making stained glass
Reading
Drawing
Building small appliances
Woodworking

You probably noticed that some of these hobbies are the kind that used to be considered girls' hobbies. That does not mean you should avoid them. But you might also try the ones that used to be thought of as boys' hobbies. I learned to hammer and saw and drill as a young girl. And when I was a young adult, my father gave me a circular saw for one birthday and a router for another. If you love tools, you can learn how to use them. Just look around for someone who can show you how.

4. *Check out the jobs of people you know.* The parents of your friends probably work, but do you know what they do? Most of them would enjoy telling you about their work if you ask them sometime.

Mothers, your daughter would probably love to see where you work. If your workplace will allow it, make a date

---

MOTHERS:

- What job do you do?
- Describe what you do during the time you are at work.
- What do you like best about your job? What do you like least?
- Tell how you use math, reading, and writing skills in your job.

DAUGHTERS:

- List the jobs of some of the other adults you know.
- How do their jobs require reading and writing skills?

---

to do that sometime, just the two of you. Daughters, your father or friends' parents may agree to take you to their work-places, too, if you ask them.

5. *Find out more about the jobs you are interested in.* Since you probably won't know someone in *every* type of job you are interested in, you might have to get creative to find out more about these jobs. There are some simple ways to explore jobs you could someday do. Make it a habit to ask any new adults you meet about the kind of work they do. Look for books about careers at your school or community library. Call colleges or technical schools and ask them to mail you a cata-log of their courses. Or look through the yellow pages to see what kinds of services are advertised. The people in all of these places will know about jobs that may interest you. While you are looking in the phone book, check under the heading "Career Counseling" to see if there is a career center in your town with information about schools and jobs.

One other way to find out about professional careers is to contact the local, state, or national association of that pro-fession. The American Psychological Association, for example, offers information to the public about careers in psychology. The American Bar Association will give you information about careers in law. And many other organizations offer this service. If you can't find a local listing for an organization that interests you, try calling 1-800-555-1212 to see if they offer a toll-free line, or look for a home page on the Internet. A few phone calls or stamps could get you a lot of information and open some doors to your future.

When Should You Start Working?

MANY TEENAGERS look for opportunities to get experience in the work world and to earn some money of their own. This is one way to be more responsible and independent. Working

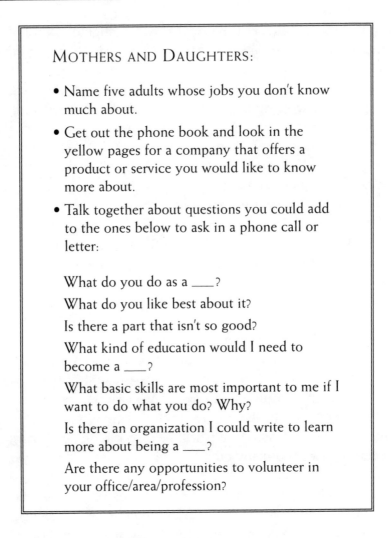

Mothers and Daughters:

- Name five adults whose jobs you don't know much about.
- Get out the phone book and look in the yellow pages for a company that offers a product or service you would like to know more about.
- Talk together about questions you could add to the ones below to ask in a phone call or letter:

What do you do as a ___?

What do you like best about it?

Is there a part that isn't so good?

What kind of education would I need to become a ___?

What basic skills are most important to me if I want to do what you do? Why?

Is there an organization I could write to learn more about being a ___?

Are there any opportunities to volunteer in your office/area/profession?

can help you learn about yourself and other people. But your parents will have some thoughts about whether and when you should take on a job. It can depend on a lot of things: how old you are, whether a parent would have to drive you to it, and how many other activities you are involved in. In a lot of ways, being a teenager is a job in itself. You learn a lot from your family, friends, and school. If you work all the time, your grades might go down, or you might not be able to participate in extracurricular activities or hobbies that can help you figure out what you want to do. And, just like your mother, you don't want work to run your life. You need to leave time for family and fun. That said, working in moderation can be a good idea. It gives you a chance to show how good you can be at getting to work on time, negotiating your work hours with a boss, and getting along with your co-workers. It is a great way to meet interesting people. And it can teach you which jobs you like and which ones you don't.

Every state has laws about how old you must be to work in places like stores and restaurants. Often you can do volunteer work at a younger age than you can work in a

---

MOTHERS AND DAUGHTERS:

Add to this list of possible places you could call to find volunteer positions:

- Hospitals (visiting children, providing information, etc.)
- Offices (filing or copying)
- Habitat for Humanity (helping to build houses; fixing food)
- Veterinarian's office or animal shelter (clean kennels and stables; feed or groom animals)
- Soup kitchen or homeless shelter (play with children; serve food)
- Theater or performing arts center (ushering, being in plays)
- Churches
- Summer camps (assisting with activities)

paid position. In fact, no matter how old you are, if you don't need the money, you may find better opportunities to experience different fields of work in a volunteer position. As a volunteer, you can work in places where people do the kind of work you are interested in, even if you can't do the work itself. Volunteers are very important to your community, and doing unpaid work is in no way less important than working for money. It is a great way to find out what it is like to work in a field and to make an important contribution at the same time.

As a preteen you may not be able to work in an official job or volunteer position just yet. But if you want work experience or spending money, you might be surprised at the other ways you can get it. There probably are jobs you can do around the house that are not part of your regular chores. Or you might offer to mow your neighbor's lawn or walk her dog. Even if you aren't able to baby-sit on your own, you could offer to be a parent's helper. You could look after children in your house or someone else's—with an adult around —to give the parent a break and learn how to baby-sit. You could read to your little sister or brother or volunteer to tutor a child who is having trouble with her schoolwork. Even these jobs can start you on your way to knowing what you want to do later in life.

MOTHERS AND DAUGHTERS:

- Is there a job you would *not* want? Why?
- What would you be if you could try something out for a day or a week?
- What job would you try next?

EPILOGUE

Do a Little Dreaming

CONGRATULATIONS, you have covered a lot of territory together in this book! By taking the time from your busy lives to read it and do the exercises together, you have sent an important message to each other about how much you care. You have laid an important foundation that can be strengthened even more in the years ahead. As things come up in the future, you may want to read some of the chapters again. I hope you will take every opportunity to learn more about each other—to listen to each other's opinions, ideas, and dreams. When you wonder what the other is thinking, need information, or have strong feelings about something, I hope you will talk to each other, or even make up your own communication exercises.

Not that things will always be easy. Relationships never are. But with a little bit of effort, you can both enjoy these years. Mothers get to go back over their lives, think about what they have learned, and model how to live. They get to watch their daughter turn into a competent, confident young adult. Daughters get to use their mother as a resource for information and guidance—to learn from her successes and mistakes. And they get to choose who and what they want to be from a world of possibilities. *Listen* carefully to each other, try not to get too upset about the little things, and realize that although you are two separate people who are going to have different opinions about things, you both have the same goal —to face adolescence, and the rest of life, as a team.

So share your thoughts and dreams without embarrassment. Follow different interests as you go along. And be aware of who and what is influencing you as a female in today's world. Think about where you want to go from here, and look at things from each other's eyes. The time you share now will be important to both of you for years to come.

MOTHERS AND DAUGHTERS:

- Name three things you learned about your mother/daughter.
- What else would you like to know about her?
- When will you have this kind of talk again?
- What questions do you want to discuss then?
- What will you do differently because you read this book?
- What do you appreciate most about your mother/daughter?